PASSING NOTES TO STRANGERS

*Craft Messages That Connect,
in Business and in Life*

David Flynn

For Liz, Presley, and Beckett.
I really hope this works.

CONTENTS

INTRODUCTION

"If it wasn't hard, everyone would do it. It's the hard that makes it great."

– JIMMY DUGAN (TOM HANKS), A LEAGUE OF THEIR OWN

"NOBODY GETS BACK TO ME"

Passing notes to strangers, cold outreach, cold connections—it can all be a real drag.

LinkedIn, X, email, and snail mail may all seem like the domain of business development, but that's not the case. Most of the people who pick up this book will be in some sort of sales role, but the truth is we're all passing notes to strangers.

We start as kids in school, but it doesn't stop there. As you grow up, you pass notes to college admissions and potential employers.

Once you land a job, you pass them even more. Emails to peers, other organizations, or the new VP. Slack messages to the technology team, finance, or training and development.

Entrepreneurs pass them when they're looking to recruit talent or increase funding.

Teachers pass them to communicate with students,

parents, and their community.

Nonprofits pass them to retain sponsors and increase participation.

And of course, for those in sales, marketing, and business development, you pass notes for a living. The information that was once relayed through door-to-door conversations, telephone solicitation, and face-to-face meetings is increasingly being funneled through other media, which means you need to upgrade your messaging.

So, what is this book and who is it for?

This is a playbook. A manual. The notes and techniques I've learned during twenty years in business development. I've applied a little polish, a bit of narrative. I even checked the spelling.

This book is an answer to the thing I hear most in my role as a sales leader.

"Nobody gets back to me."

It's not just for sales and marketing though—it's for anyone who uses writing to package what they do and how they contribute. It's for the people who want to write in a way that will connect with the people they seek to serve.

I think that's most of us.

A FORMULA
THAT WORKS

Passing notes isn't that complex. We've been doing it for a long time. My first girlfriend used a note to ask me out. The note said, "Check yes or no," and it worked.

She dumped me with a note as well. "I think we should just be friends."

Passing notes as a kid can be risky. Teachers don't want distractions in the classroom, but do we have a choice? If we have something to say, and they won't let us say it, we've got to write it down and pass it around.

If you get caught, it might mean detention. Or worse. They might read it for the whole class to hear.

Your friend could intercept it too. They act cool, pretend they'll pass it along, and boom, they crack that sucker open and start reading, giggling, and pointing fingers. They might share it with a few more classmates so the group can give you a hard time during recess.

Ah, memories.

We learn from these experiences that notes can be a powerful thing.

"Do you like Susie?? Check yes or no."

Shoot, I don't know. I think she's nice.

Good notes have a somewhat formulaic structure. You may have heard of it.

AIDA: Attention, Interest, Desire, and Action.

Attention: Hey, I like you.

Okay, you've got my attention! A little forward, but at least I'm not left wondering if we're just friends.

Interest: I'm headed to the basketball game after school.

That's talking my language. I'm interested in basketball for sure. Oh, and you. I'm interested in you too.

Desire: Lots of cool people will be there, and it's going to be a lot of fun.

Fun? Fun sounds fun. Let's do it. Let's have fun.

Action: Wanna go? Yes, or no? I'll drive.

Okay, that's an easy action. Yes, please.

But I kind of know Susie. She's not a total stranger.

When we pass notes to strangers for business, charity, or public service, it's not quite as easy. Does the same AIDA formula work?

The notes we pass to classmates in our youth come bundled with social pressures, an *expectation* that recipients will respond. If not during class, maybe on the playground, in the halls, or after school.

Out in the wild, people don't feel that same pressure to respond, and they just delete things that don't catch their attention.

Strangers aren't held to any social standard to respond or even be polite. They don't know us. They don't want to know us. And they're not going to be forced to see us during chemistry. That's a big social difference.

Asking them to "Check yes or no" might not be enough to overcome the stranger danger these recipients can feel, and this book will cover the tools you need to overcome these hurdles.

With added complexity, many people have chosen to turn the volume up. More power! The people passing notes are sending too many, and there's no way for our audience to respond to everything. We're our own worst enemy. What if every kid in school passed you a "yes or no" note every day? You'd never be able to respond to all of them, and you'd never be able to trust that they were sincere.

Sounds a little like spam because it is spam.

Passing notes to strangers isn't so different from passing notes in school. Please don't tell me you printed seventy-three copies of your note asking [insert fellow student] to the dance. Seriously. Say it. You didn't print seventy-three copies, right?

Of course not. First, you figured out who you'd like to go with and why.

You said hello. You investigated, talked to some of their friends to see if you had anything in common. If it seemed like a match, then you crafted that note.

You tried to catch their attention, flowers and hearts. You added a little flair like the server at TGI Fridays.

Once they opened that eye-catching, perfectly folded

notebook paper, it was getting their interest and desire, no doubt about it. *"It's going to be a great time, we will go with your friends Johnny and Jennifer, and then catch the laser show afterwards."*

Yep, that will do it.

And of course, that call to action is as easy and safe as can be. *"Check yes or no. I'll pick you up at 6:00PM."* That's pretty much a done deal.

Hopefully this all sounds familiar. I'm sure it's buried in some deep recesses of your mind. While you read this book, do your best to remember and reinstate some of the basics of being a human. Apply these same rules and frameworks to the people you're working with now.

That's what passing notes to strangers is all about.

I HATE COLD CALLS

I hate cold calls, and so does everyone else. There, I said it. I hate cold calls. I hate awkward networking events. I hate in-person impromptu referrals. And I hate elevator pitches.

Interrupting people at their desks and at dinner feels rude. Butting in, listening in, and sliding in on other people's conversations feels slimy.

Twenty years ago, when I was getting started in sales, I was looking for another way. Something had to be better than pounding the phones.

I found email.

And now LinkedIn, X, Discord, and the rest.

I wondered if email could be used in the same way snail mail was used in the past. The same way advertising and copywriting were leveraged.

I started reading and writing and borrowing ideas, putting them into play. I wanted to provide the details about my service to people who needed it, in a way that worked for them. I wanted to do that on their timeline and on their platform of choice. I wanted to meet them where they wanted to buy, with what they needed.

And I've had great success doing it.

Strangely enough, the information I found useful for passing notes wasn't available in one place. I'd make recommendations to my team, and the list of blogs, podcasts, and books was too long. It included a lot of wonderful information but was bundled with things they didn't need. New hires, in addition to their standard onboarding, were feeling overwhelmed with my stack of homework on copywriting, negotiation, psychology, and writing.

So, I cobbled together my notes from these various sources. Enough of the theory to get the point across, enough of the real world to make it stick.

That document might have been where it ended, but something else happened. The world changed. People stopped answering their phones. They stopped saying hello. The networking events died off, and the way we connect shifted.

Video has exploded, but so has written communication. Call your kids. They'll hit ignore and then immediately text you back. They prefer text, and these are people who love you. How's that going to work out with a perfect stranger you're interrupting with a sales call?

Cold calls are the pits. Buyer, seller, doesn't matter—nobody likes them. But the inconvenient truth is that at some point you'll need to connect with someone you don't know. Someone who's cold. And what I've found is that people prefer if you pass them a note.

CHAPTER ONE: WHY DO WE DO IT?

"The secret of getting ahead is getting started."

– MARK TWAIN

IT'S NECESSARY

If you want to do anything, you've got to get started. That means getting yourself and your message in front of those you seek to serve. They won't simply stumble upon you while surfing the web. Search engine optimization will not land customers at your door.

What you need is momentum.

We learn in science that an object in motion stays in motion unless acted on by an external force. Likewise, an object at rest will remain at rest unless acted on by an external force.

Notice the theme? It's an external force.

If you're just getting started, you need to take action to get things moving.

Let's think about SpaceX for a moment, because rockets are cooler than cold emails.

It takes 7.2 million pounds (about 3.5 million kilograms) of thrust to reach escape velocity and leave earth's gravitational pull.[1] That's what's required to reach nearly 18,000 miles (about 28,968 kilometers) per hour.[2] Once the rocket is moving, it releases its boosters. Next, it reaches low orbit, and then outer space, where it takes much less energy to keep going. Over 90 percent of the rocket's total weight is fuel, and most of that is used in the eight minutes between the earth's surface and space.

Are you picking up on the analogy?

If you're going to start anything, you'll need to spend a huge amount of energy up front to get going and build momentum. In most organizations that means cold outreach to build relationships.

DO COLD EMAILS EVEN WORK?

Great question.

Yes. They work.

I didn't write this book just to end it after 1,879 words with, "Sorry, this is useless. Just go home." I should leave it there and move on, but I feel obligated to provide a bit more detail in exchange for your time and attention.

To be clear: Cold emails, instant messages (IMs), direct messages (DMs), and any type of cold outreach can and will work.

But you need to take some time to get it right.

Identify your audience and tailor your messaging. Understand and articulate your value and deliver it at each interaction. Your written content is an important part of your broader sales, marketing, and networking campaign.

You won't get 100 percent on this test, and you don't need to. If your response rates trend down, or don't hit benchmarks, you should improve the quality of your campaign.

You hear that?

I didn't say increase your speed or volume; I said improve quality. Your content and your offerings need to be high quality and a match for the audience, or they'll never make the impact you're looking for.

Will all your responses turn into business? No way. Not everyone needs what you're selling. Get them to respond, and you can have that conversation and start a relationship. That's the goal when passing notes to strangers.

We're not pretending to be some far-flung family member incarcerated overseas, and we're not trying to get prospects to PayPal us twenty bucks from a single email.

What we're trying to do is connect.

Express to our prospect what our product or service does and how it might help them. We're trying to connect with them about our business or nonprofit, to see if it meets their criteria.

This is about getting started with the long game, not closing a quick sale with copywriting tricks.

But we should talk a bit more about tricks.

QUICK QUESTION

Why did you open this book?

Was it because you wanted to increase open rates, conversion rates, and closing rates? Those are common answers. Along with increased contacts and activity and connections. Many sales books cover those items in detail, and they have a spin toward trickery.

They call them *tactics*.

The fact of the matter is that "quick question" as a subject line is one of the most effective tactics in the business. Effective at what, exactly?

Effective at getting people to open your note.

It'll work with a man on the street as well. Someone approaches you in Pike Place Market with a *quick question*, and you might be willing to hear them out. The first time. You'd expect them to ask which way to the pier, how far to the stadiums, or if you've ever had Beecher's famous Mac & Cheese. For any of those *quick questions*, you'll deliver their answer quickly and go about your day.

But all too often they follow with a larger ask.

It's not quick or a question. Maybe they want to tell

you about some hard luck. Maybe they have a talent. They want money for a joke, or a riddle, or push-ups, or a song. I've seen it all, but I haven't seen many *quick questions* that live up to their billing.

These tactics have an impact on trust and our willingness to listen to quick questions in the future.

You can kick things off with a trick or a tactic and see if that will improve your open rates. If your copywriting is slick and savvy, and your product is helpful, or your service is needed, they'll read on, captivated by your value. In the end, they'll make a purchase.

But most of the time, these questions are quick to ask and quite tiresome to answer.

No customer or coworker appreciates being tricked or having their attention coerced, even if the outcome is positive.

Most people don't buy from tricksters, just out of principle, if they have a choice in the matter.

So, I have a quick question for you. And you can take your time answering it. Can we turn our focus toward the customer for a moment? Can we look to make a positive impact on their work and their lives? Can the goal be to make progress together instead of playing games?

To do that, we need to engage in honest dialogue. When we're passing notes to strangers, we need to focus on delivering a relevant and helpful message in a way that serves them. We need to make life easier for them.

It's not about tricking people into opening your note, fooling them into meeting, or distracting them from their work.

It's about delivering what they need, when they need

it.

If that's interesting to you, I hope the pages that follow deliver what you need, when you need it.

IT'S NOT EASY

Passing notes to strangers is hard as hell. Emails or IMs, you don't know them, they don't know you, and once it's sent—it's sent.

You don't get to say it with a smile and a wink.

You don't get to backtrack with a "What I really meant was..."

It's gone. That ship has sailed. I hope you like the cargo.

What they read is what you write—plus the inner voice they have running at the time. That makes getting through to them with your true intention quite difficult.

We read with our own inflection. It takes a capable writer to provide all the context and clues that support our message, not just the words and the information. We need to supply the emotion and intent as well, or they'll be scratching their heads thinking, *what did they mean by that?*

If the last person to reach out with a solicitation was a real jerk, guess what? They'll read your thoughtful note with that person's voice and character in mind.

Capable writing takes some practice. Some study.

Because getting the attention of people who don't have much to give is difficult. That's the definition of a scarce resource.

It's not going to be easy, and that's exactly why this skill is so valuable.

THE CHOICE IS YOURS

Let's get started.

We'll walk through the four Cs: collecting, connecting, crafting, and caring. If you can commit (the fifth C) to those basics, you can improve your writing and improve your outcomes.

Remember, these people aren't sitting there waiting for their first email. They have no innate desire to read your scripts and templates and don't really want you in their inbox.

That leads us to the first part of our journey. Why *are* you in their inbox?

If you can't answer that question, take a walk. You need to do some thinking.

I know what is going through your mind. *Dave, this sounds hard. I just want to send a template email to 1,000 of my best leads and see what happens.*

If that's you, go do it.

You can spray and pray. You can play the numbers

game. I've seen people survive that way. They ruffled some feathers along the way, and I'm sure they had some embarrassing moments, but they made it work. They channeled Wayne Gretzky, "You miss all the shots you don't take," but they should have gone with John Wooden, "Never mistake activity for achievement."

Wooden has more championships.

If you'd like to push numbers and see what happens, please pass this book along to a child in need. We won't cover that method here.

This approach is slower, but it saves time. It's harder, but it's less work.

It's efficient. And I like efficient.

WHAT ARE WE UP AGAINST?

Failure. There's always failure. But that's mostly in your head. If you're just getting started, how far can you fall?

X.com is full of posts mocking salespeople and entrepreneurs. They're mocking the bad actors. The lazy approach. That's not you.

People will even post the terrible emails they get. They'll hashtag #bestoflinkedin and maybe, if you're lucky, they'll redact your name.

Hello –

Hope your day is going well. I wanted to touch base regarding your 2024 initiatives. Can you carve out 15 minutes later this week to connect?

Sincerely,

Salesperson of the Year

And those are just the emails that get opened, so the sender has done something right. Sadly, most of our notes just go directly to the delete folder.

How do we avoid being ignored, or worse, being

ridiculed?

First, we need to have empathy and understanding and put ourselves in the recipient's shoes. Remember the walk you took to think about why you're reaching out? What did you come up with?

Let me guess:

My boss told me I need more sales activity.

They looked nice on LinkedIn.

I had an email address for once.

Sure, these are *reasons*. Bad reasons, but reasons all the same. What is the recipient's reason for meeting?

We don't know them, so how the heck do we get started? Great question. Let's find the answer.

GET THE BALL ROLLING

Passing notes to strangers is a way to connect. It's the bridge between what you do and the people you serve.

Email is powerful and ubiquitous. It can be your best lead generation tool, or it can be spam. Your choice. When cold emails are done right, when they connect with the right audience, both sides are happy they took the time.

The goal isn't to land a deal; it's to connect with someone. Maybe. If the need is there and the timing is right.

But it's got to be good, and most of the time it's got to be quick. Most people only scan an email for a few seconds before deciding to delete or keep reading.

Get them to keep reading.

Passing notes, cold email—they're for getting the ball rolling, getting a little momentum, getting just the slightest toe hold so you can stay engaged and take the next step.

That's it. That's the goal.

PERFECT STRANGERS

How do we kick off a new relationship? We need to connect with perfect strangers.

Perfect strangers are people with no previous association. Completely unknown.

But before we talk about perfect strangers in business, I want to talk about the 80s sitcom *Perfect Strangers*.

Balki Bartokomous (Bronson Pinchot) moves to Chicago from his humble roots as a shepherd in Mypos, a mostly made-up country in the Mediterranean. Where will young Balki stay? With his distant cousin Larry Appleton (Mark Linn-Baker), who just happens to have moved into an apartment with an extra room.

Classic fish-out-of-water hysteria follows as Larry teaches Balki about city life in the United States.

But don't forget the big hurdle that was removed to get Balki in the door with Larry.

They were cousins.

Strangers, yes, but they had a massive thing in

common: shared DNA. And that's the first lesson in connecting with perfect strangers.

Find some shared DNA.

Please don't consider this a cop-out. It doesn't need to be literal DNA, but something shared and important to both of you. Package that DNA up with some skillful writing, and then follow up in a timely, helpful, and interesting manner.

That sounds like a good game plan to me.

How do we collect that information? How do we find shared DNA? That is what we'll discuss next.

Think of this next section as scaffolding for your outreach. Don't focus on what you don't have in common; focus on what you do and build from that.

If you do, those perfect strangers will open their door to you, just like Larry did for his cousin Balki.

CHAPTER TWO: COLLECTING

"If I don't turn over the rocks, I won't see the dots. If I don't collect the dots, I can't connect the dots."

– DANNY MEYER

STALK BEFORE YOU TALK

We need to collect some information to get started. We need to find that shared DNA. This process requires some stalking.

Yes, I'm telling you to cyberstalk them.

No, not like a psycho. Just to understand what they do and how you can help. This is the good kind of cyberstalking you don't hear about on the news.

You need to collect this information to warm up your pitch. We're a few chapters in now, but I've got news for you. Cold outreach stinks, and it doesn't work. Let's warm it up a bit.

Don't act like you don't already do this. Your kid gets a new Little League coach, and you're hitting the Google machine to see what they do and who they know. This is just the world we live in.

You need to know about them, where they went to school, what they're interested in, what they're working on, and what's important to them.

I know what you're saying.

"Why do I need to know that? I've got my talking points, I've got my script, let's start hitting them up."

Please, for the love of all that's good and holy, ditch the script. The world has enough bad actors.

You need to do the homework first so you can offer value. Hard to offer value if you go in blind. Spend some time on this, do the homework, and find some information on your prospects. Once you understand their needs, make it clear to them what value they'll get by reading and responding to your outreach.

You get good intelligence for business the same way you do for the Little League coach. Follow on social, set Google alerts, and read their blog. Information is more abundant than ever before, so get creative and do some preparation. If I were you, I'd collect as much relevant information as I could before firing off any notes.

WHO IS IT FOR?

Who is it for? That is the first question you need to answer. And the answer will guide your work to find an audience.

Malcolm Gladwell tells a story about meeting his reader in the wild.[3]

"Years ago, I sat down on an airplane next to a guy who happened to be reading one of my books. His job was to go around the country opening Trader Joe's. He was coming from New York, they were opening a store in Brooklyn, and he'd just been in Brooklyn for a month.

He lived in Atlanta, had two kids, and was thirty-eight years old. Business school degree. We had this lovely chat and I realized, *Oh that's my reader*, and every time I'm stuck, I think about him. It's for him."

The man told Gladwell, "I'm very busy, I teach Sunday school, I'm a coach in my kid's Little League, and I have this job which is very demanding. I have time to read three books a year." That is when it hit Gladwell, "He's chosen one of mine; I'm one of his three, which is a phenomenally flattering thing, and I realized if I could keep being one of his three books every year, then I will succeed."

Gladwell says, "I think about him all the time. It's insanely liberating to know, that's what it's for, for that guy on the airplane."

Of course, Gladwell's reader is another way of saying Gladwell's buyer. His customer.

Malcolm Gladwell and J.K. Rowling have different readers. Sure, they have some overlap—I'm part of that group. I read everything from both. That said, the moment Rowling tries to cross over, once Harry Potter starts investigating the unintended psychological consequences of the wizarding caste system through the lens of a Muggle's cognitive bias—I'm probably out.

Both authors know this. It's called knowing your customer.

Knowing your customer (KYC) is key to growing a business. It brings clarity to both sides, the seller and the buyer. Gladwell understands, *It's for him*, and he understands the importance of the buyer seeing *The Tipping Point*, or *Talking to Strangers*, and thinking, *It's for me*.

Don't wait to stumble across someone on an airplane. Proactively go to the audience you want to serve, and work to understand them better.

If you don't know who they are, how will you know when you've found them? You might already have fish in a barrel. If you don't recognize that, you'll head down to the bait shop instead of draining off the water.

Patagonia founder Yvon Chouinard built his company to serve a customer he knew well.

Himself.

And his dirtbag climbing buddies.

As the company grew past climbing, into outdoor sports of all kinds, it needed to be more deliberate about staying in contact with its customers.

"We know that for customers as well as for ourselves, the most valued advice we can receive is that from a trusted friend," Chouinard said. He knew that Patagonia's customers "respect the opinions of pros or experts like outdoor instructors, climbing guides, fishing guides, or river outfitters."[4]

So instead of commercials on prime time, Patagonia spread by word of mouth. And it spread through the Patagonia Ambassadors, a group of like-minded professionals who not only loved the equipment, but also loved and cherished Patagonia's mission.

First look to understand the customer, and then meet them where they are.

What did Chouinard know about these customers and how they shopped?

He said, "If there is one common trait to all outdoor people, it's the fact that they do not spend their free time aimlessly shopping. If he or she is going to drive for twenty minutes to a store, it's to buy certain needed items; it's not to be entertained like the Bloomingdale's customer. And I can tell you these people are going to be angry if the store doesn't have what they want."

Smart people, with money, but not much time. Sounds like an ideal customer. They don't enjoy the shopping process. They want what they need, so they can get back to doing what they love. Going outside.

Do you know that much about the people you're trying

to connect with?

Young sales executives will think their customer is anyone who'll talk to them. That is some late-night-at-the-club kind of desperation.

Large retailers think their customer is anyone they have an email for. Costco is still sending me one-size-fits-all advertisements even though they know every purchase I've ever made at their stores.

Customers who are short on time and attention are asked to sit for PowerPoint pitches that are unrelated and undifferentiated.

Technology is being used as leverage to scale, but sometimes when you cast a wider net, you catch rubber boots.

Get sharp. Get more precise. That means you can't simply push out more emails to more people and expect better results. You need to understand them like Gladwell and Chouinard do.

An unaimed arrow rarely hits a target.

If I were you, I'd make a sketch of your target audience. Seriously, do it. With crayons, if you must. Who is your customer? The one who buys your product or service quickly and consistently without shaking you down on the price. The one who invests in similar businesses and has the money, passion, and experience to support you?

Is it a business or a consumer?

Where are they located?

Education? Age?

What business are they in?

Small business or enterprise?

Family? Single?

What problem are they trying to solve?

What is their desired outcome?

How do you help them reach their goals? Now confirm it with data. Be cautious of customer interviews that don't match buying patterns. Everyone thinks augmented reality is cool, and yet nobody is walking the streets with smart glasses. If you're raising money, double check the large pledges are coming from people with a history of signing big checks.

It's like that trick question during your physical: "How much alcohol do you drink?" There are two answers: the truth, and the number you tell your doctor.

The way to understand what people will buy is to look at what they do buy.

So, before you go passing notes, sketch out the ideal member of your audience, validate with data and experience, and then keep providing the things they need.

When you get off track, when you're not sure of the next step to take, circle back to your homework. Take another look at the sketch you made of the reader, the buyer, the investor, and it'll give you clarity on that important question.

Who is it for?

Malcolm knows. Yvon does too. But do you?

PARETO'S LAW

Commonly known as the 80/20 rule, Pareto's Law was created by the Italian economist Vilfredo Pareto, who noticed that approximately 80 percent of Italy's land was owned by 20 percent of the population. He then went on to see that the same power law distribution applied to many other fields.

Pareto's Law states that 80 percent of outputs comes from 20 percent of inputs. Eighty percent of your results come from 20 percent of your work.[5]

Here is how it works:

Twenty percent of computer bugs cause 80 percent of user issues.

Eighty percent of sales come from 20 percent of clients.

Twenty percent of donors contribute 80 percent of funds.

Eighty percent of income goes to 20 percent of the population.

Twenty percent of hazards cause 80 percent of injuries.

In other words, a small portion of inputs cause most of the outputs.

Focus on what is driving your results. If a particular product is getting all the responses, lean into that. If a particular segment of the audience is driving all the sales, lean into that. If a particular template or tone in your outreach is driving all the donations, lean into that.

Like baseball, the failure rate with passing notes to strangers is massive. Don't just go up to the plate and swing wildly. Have a plan. And inform your plan with data from your results.

If I were you, I would be very observant, track my outreach diligently, and understand what is working. Understand the 20 percent that's driving 80 percent of your results.

And then I'd double down with that niche.

THE RICHES ARE IN THE NICHES

Once you understand who it's for, you can start to build out your list of targets.

This will take some focus.

Remember, less is more. You want to identify the key people who can help drive your work forward.

You want to find your niche. Your service fills a need, something that's essential and desired but not for everyone. You need to find the group that's the best match for what you provide. The 20 percent that will account for most of your results.

Most people want thousands of leads. But why knock on every door in town when you know the buyers are in the next city over?

Even Gary Halbert, one of the best copywriters of all time, emphasized the importance of trimming down your list.[6] His work was during the days of direct mail, but the practice is the same. You can't send letters to everyone in the phone book—that would be a waste of time and effort. You need to narrow the field.

Affluent neighborhoods.

Near the water.

With multiple automobiles.

That sounds like a better target for a new boat than the population at large, right?

These are demographics you have been able to pull for the last fifty years, and now you can be more precise than ever before. But instead of using the technology to be more precise, we're using it to leverage more volume. And that's all backward.

We need an accurate drone strike instead of carpet bombing the whole jungle.

The tools change all the time, and each generation is better than the last.

Seriously, when I started selling technology staffing, I would drive from office building to office building to look for new prospects. After meetings, I would look around town for new business parks. If I found a full parking lot, I'd assume the business were doing well, so I would go inside to investigate. Like a private detective, I would ask around and write down all the businesses listed in the directory.

Did any sound like they were high-tech? That would be a bonus. They might need technology staffing.

I would pop my head into each door and ask if they had an IT (information technology) manager on site. That would be our buyer. Maybe.

Sometimes the receptionist would ask, "What's an IT?" and other times they would say, "Like computers?"

"Yes. Like computers, ma'am."

If they had someone who knew what we were talking about, we would have the meeting on the spot, right in the lobby.

If not, we'd try to get a referral and call back.

No matter how you slice it, that was a colossal waste of human life. Hours and days spent walking the halls and talking with people who had no interest.

Compare that to LinkedIn and ZoomInfo, and you'll see why I'm not fussy when it comes to tools for finding targets. How you track them matters even less. Customer relationship management (CRM) software or Excel—take your pick. It'll depend on how many people are in your market, but you could do this with a yellow sticky note if you've properly identified the top few decision makers.

I'll say it again: less is more.

Try some different tools and stick with what you like. Follow people and industries on social and go deep down the rabbit hole.

It's easier than you think. Just keep an open and curious mind, and you'll find your people. But finding your people and their contact information is the easy part; it's also the part that holds people up. They use it as an excuse for not acting.

In the classic scene from *Glengarry Glenn Ross*, Shelley Levene (Jack Lemmon) tells Blake (Alex Baldwin), "The leads are weak." He wants the stack of new leads. Blake disagrees and tells Shelley, "The leads aren't weak; you're weak," and he's probably right.

Find the high-quality targets, and do a high-quality job getting in front of them. None of that takes innovative technology, massive markets, or a big stack of new leads from corporate.

Always be collecting information, reaching out, staying consistent, and you'll have more than enough pipeline.

As you compile a list of targets and prospects, take notes on why they might want to meet with you, and file that in whatever system you're using, CRM or otherwise.

Remember, nobody cares about you. They're busy doing what they do. They get hundreds if not thousands of emails and notifications every week. They have defaulted to tuning you out. They care about themselves and their work.

To get an audience with them, you need to make it easy to understand the value you provide. That is what they need to know.

How can you stand out? How can you get them to tune in and focus on your note and then act on it?

It's back to that shared DNA and a concept called uncommon commonalities.

THE BURIEN DROP

We all think Die Hard is the greatest Christmas movie of all time, and Pearl Jam is the greatest band.

Nothing uncommon there.

But what if we had something in common with just a few people? What would that conversation look like?

That indie band you follow? Have you ever bumped into someone else who followed them on their epic 2009 West Coast tour? That is a much more powerful connection than *growing up on the Rolling Stones*.

Have you ever run into a fellow American when traveling overseas? Hoboken and Huntsville never felt so close.

Adam Grant calls these cross-sections uncommon commonalities.

In his book *Give and Take*, Grant explains that the similarities we value are rare ones. Uncommon commonalities draw people together. They make people feel like they're fitting in and standing out at the same time.[7]

Grant put this into practice with his own cold

outreach. He says, "When I cold-emailed Zappos.com CEO Tony Hsieh, my first instinct was to mention that we attended the same college. After realizing that thousands of people share that connection with him, I looked for uncommon commonalities. I ended up writing that I first learned about him when my college roommate followed in his footsteps to run the Quincy Grille."

Mentioning the Quincy Grille, a student-run concession stand at Quincy House, told Tony they went to the same school, stayed in the same dorm, and ran in the same circle. It is a much more powerful connection.

The lesson: having something in common isn't nearly enough.

I Was Born In Kowloon Bay:

In the nineties comedy *Wayne's World*, Benjamin (Rob Lowe) makes an impression on Cassandra (Tia Carrere), a Chinese immigrant turned budding rock star, with his knowledge of her home country. A very uncommon commonality in the group she runs with at clubs around Chicago.

Benjamin asks the group, "Who wants Chinese takeout?" and checks with Cassandra to see if she would like to order.

Cassandra defers to Benjamin, "Whatever you order will be fine," and he calls in the order using authentic Cantonese. Cassandra is understandably impressed, as is Wayne (Mike Myers).

Benjamin explains that he picked up some Cantonese during his travels through eastern Asia, before mentioning that Cassandra sounds like she's "from

Kowloon Bay as opposed to Hong Kong."

Blown away, Cassandra exclaims, "I was born in Kowloon Bay!"

That is the powerful connection.

These uncommon commonalities are where we can build bonds where none previously existed. They help people quickly build trust, feel safe, and let their guard down.

I grew up in Burien, Washington, a small city just south of Seattle. Because it's smaller, it's also more uncommon, and that's a good thing. Being from Burien is more unique. It is one of those *if you know you know* kind of places that makes it worth mentioning if there is the slightest hint of a connection. So, I leverage that whenever I can.

The moment I bring up my hometown is what my coworkers call "The Burien Drop." I'll get IMs from them during the call.

"Four minutes and thirty-seven seconds. A new record."

"There it is, the Burien Drop."

"Wow, did you just take the conversation from nearshoring data analytics work to talking about Mexican restaurants in Burien?"

Highlighting uncommon commonalities is the best way to catch a person's attention.

Where are you from, what are you involved in, what are you interested in that's uncommon?

I know what you're thinking: *Dave, help me. I'm not from Burien, and I don't know Cantonese. How will I make friends using the uncommon commonalities technique?*

I have good news. It works for so many things, and all it takes is awareness and curiosity. It can be done in several ways besides mentioning your hometown.

If I see a LinkedIn profile picture in the mountains, you'd better believe I'm latching on to that and trying to steer the conversation towards backpacking. Something I enjoy in my free time. It's not exactly America's pastime.

If I see a background in education, I'm talking about my parents who were both teachers.

And like Adam Grant, if we attended the same school, I'll find out if they're from the same year, same fraternity, same major, or same activities.

There's no wrong way to do this. Just drill down on what you know and find something novel.

"We're both from New York" isn't the same as "We're both from Brooklyn."

"We both play cricket" might not mean much in India, but it means a lot when you live in Savannah.

The ability to connect with people on these less common frequencies is critical. It quickly breaks down barriers and builds relationships.

Robert Cialdini summarizes this phenomenon, saying, "We like people who are like us." Cialdini also points out that because people are more likely to search for separations, to identify how we're different rather than how we're the same, putting an effort toward highlighting similarities is "a way to prompt harmonious interactions."[8]

In other words, calling attention to commonalities is a

good idea.

So do it.

If I were you, I'd take my list of qualified prospects and targets, and for each one, I'd try to find some commonality, something you share, and the more uncommon that something is, the better chance you have of catching their attention. Take note of these things, and customize your notes to emphasize where the two of you have crossed paths in life.

"I hope you're enjoying the summer."

"With the school year quickly approaching..."

These are pleasantries that get looked over on their way to the delete folder. We need an upgrade that'll catch someone's attention.

"Easy way to help fellow Debate Club Captain from Chattanooga State" is a much more uncommon way to connect.

Anyone and everyone at the water cooler can talk about the Seahawks or the latest *Mission Impossible*. You want to work your way toward being a bit more uncommon.

THE BEN FRANKLIN EFFECT

You wouldn't help someone you didn't like, would you? You might, if they asked you in the right way.

And once you'd helped them, you'd have to resolve that inner conflict with yourself. *Did I just help that guy?* Which would then improve your opinion of that person, because again, you wouldn't help someone you didn't like. Would you?

Wild, huh?

A person who has already performed a favor for you is more likely to do you another favor, even if they don't really like you, simply based on the first favor.[9]

They're bought in.

In his autobiography, Ben Franklin explains how he dealt with the animosity of a rival legislator when he served in the Pennsylvania Assembly:

"Having heard that he had in his library a certain very scarce and curious book, I wrote a note to him, expressing my desire of perusing that book, and requesting he would do me the favor of lending it to me for a few days. He sent it immediately, and I returned it in about a week with another note, expressing strongly my sense of the favor. When we next met in the House, he spoke to me (which he had never done before), and with great civility; and he ever after manifested a readiness to serve me on all occasions, so that we became great friends, and our friendship continued to his death."[10]

If you know they have rare books, that's a terrific way to improve a relationship, but how does it play out in the real world?

The Ben Franklin effect was discussed in Dale Carnegie's bestselling book *How to Win Friends and Influence People.* Carnegie interprets the request for favor as "a subtle but effective form of flattery."[11]

When we ask someone for a favor, we suggest they have value. It could be a particular skill, information, or a book. They have something we don't. That can feel good. It's a sign of respect. Our willingness to admit that we need what they have raises their opinion of us and makes them more willing to help. They see a new commonality and enjoy the feeling of admiration.

When you approach a coworker you don't have the best relationship with and say, "You're a great writer. Do you mind giving my email a quick read?" you're breaking down a barrier with them. You're giving them a compliment, stroking their ego, and if they agree, it'll also improve the chances that they'll do more favors in the future.

They're feeling good about themselves while doing you a favor, and that can be habit-forming. They'll start to see you in a more positive light because they helped you. They wouldn't help someone who was terrible, would they? No. They did you a favor, and now they might do another because it felt so good the last time around.

If I were you, I'd include the Ben Franklin effect in my arsenal when passing notes to strangers. I'd ask them for small, easy, specific, and unique favors first, and then circle back with a larger ask down the line.

CHAPTER THREE: CONNECTING

"The easiest thing is to react. The second easiest thing is to respond. But the hardest thing is to initiate."

– SETH GODIN

SHOW 'EM YOU KNOW 'EM

Passing notes to strangers is much easier if we can make ourselves familiar. They still don't know us, but they know of us. They recognize us or have heard of us. If they've seen us around town or on the internet, we can avoid them putting their defenses up and allow us to get our message across.

Listen, learn, like, link—it all works. Take your pick, or dabble in all of them.

What we want to do, before we dial up that killer email, is put the vibe out just a little bit. We want to be a familiar face when we reach out.

What many people do instead is what I call the Burgundy. In the opening scene of *Anchorman*, Ron Burgundy (Will Ferrell) is staring at himself in the dressing room mirror, saying, "I look good. I mean, really good," and then begins yelling to anyone who'll listen, "Hey, everyone! Come and see how good I look." It's a comedy, so it works, but the tragedy is that so many people attempt the same process when trying to grow their own audience.

Self-obsessed and calling for someone, anyone, to notice.

It doesn't work.

Join the conversation like you would in real life. Because this is real life. Listen, learn, add your two cents, and contribute when appropriate.

The easiest way to start is by following your prospects on social media platforms. I typically use LinkedIn and X, but you'll want to meet them on the platform of their choosing.

If you're trying to meet Mark Zuckerberg, it's going to be on Instagram, whereas Elon Musk is going to be on X. Satya Nadella is a LinkedIn guy.

The process of warming up a lead goes like this.

First Stalk, And Then Talk:

Remember the chapter on collecting? This is where we take the next step. Recall that before sending a note, you need to stalk them. Follow them, and read anything they've put on the internet.

Start on social, but blog posts and interviews can be particularly impactful. The more obscure, the better.

Blogs are long-form and typically more thought out. They're more personal than a LinkedIn post that corporate asked them to publish. Prospects will likely have fewer people spending time on longer-form content, so you'll find less of your competition doing the same thing. It's just harder, and most people shy away from harder.

You can also stalk them via community, charity, user groups, or anything else the prospect is heavily invested in. Get specific and personal. Use all that knowledge you gained while doing research and collecting information.

"Nice car" feels good, but if they rebuild cars as a hobby, mention something specific.

"Love that half-cab Bronco pickup; don't see that too often. Is that the 3.3-liter engine?"

Now their ears are perking up.

Same story with "nice house" vs "beautiful azaleas" for a green-thumbed founder you've been trying to meet.

Comment. Interact. Add value to their posts. Link back to their published work from your own website, and promote their content in a thoughtful and additive way. This strokes their ego and adds value to their work all at the same time. That's something they'll remember.

Send them research, help with small corrections to their work, and don't ask for anything in return.

Most people hurry through this stalking step, rushing into the pitch. Slow down. Be thoughtful. And play the long game.

This is the stalking and talking section. I didn't say anything about asking for bags of money yet. The goal here isn't to get frisky on the first date. The goal is to get to know them. The more info you learn, the better prepared you'll be once you get the opportunity to talk.

When the time comes, you don't want to be a perfect stranger anymore. It is much easier to do that if you are, in fact, not a stranger. Learn about them, and try to get them to notice you as well. What are they interested in? Live in Salt Lake City? Maybe it's BYU football. If they worked at *Wired* magazine, maybe they would know the founder, Kevin Kelly.

Like And Reply:

Give those hearts out and contribute to the conversation. Show support for them and their projects.

While you do that, make it easy for them to recognize you by being consistent across platforms, same profile picture and username.

Show 'em that you know 'em. It takes time and attention, but it's necessary for connecting with the people worth connecting with.

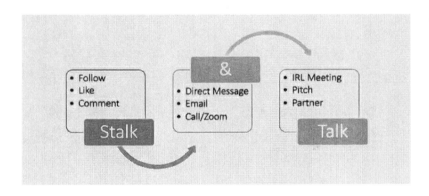

SOCIAL PROOF

University of Wisconsin football fans have a tradition. During home games, at the end of the third quarter, the stadium cranks up House of Pain's "Jump Around," and you'll never guess what happens. Everyone jumps around. They go crazy. If you've never heard the song, or don't know the tradition, you're in luck because 80,321 of your closest friends are now helping you figure out what to do.

And you jump around too.

This psychological and social phenomenon where people copy the actions of others in choosing how to behave is called social proof and was coined by Robert Cialdini in his book *Influence*.

You know what to do because other people are doing it.

The classic example of social proof is the line outside a night club or restaurant. That line, believe it or not, makes you more likely to go there.

All those great, attractive, smart people are going in. It must be awesome.

On the other side of that equation is the empty club. It must be empty for a good reason.

Bad vibe, terrible service, too many bros.

Do your prospects know what to do in the same way as Wisconsin fans? If I were you, I would find ways to include various aspects of social proof when collecting and connecting with my audience.

Testimonials and case studies from other clients.

Follower counts from social media.

Even your revenue run rate can help. If your company is growing quickly, people will wonder what they're missing, just like that big line outside the nightclub.

A new contact is going to look for ways to understand if you're credible, and they'll want to do that as quickly as possible. Social proof is like a cheat code for people to understand your credibility quickly, without doing their own research.

NOBODY LIKES NETWORKING

Nobody likes networking. It's gross. Even the social networks didn't like it, so they changed the category to social media. Networking is a charged word that brings about thoughts of awkward interactions and shallow dialogue. Speed dating for business.

In our online lives, and in our written communication, we can make things less gross.

Comment, like, ask genuine questions, offer something of yourself, and you can warm things up before you reach out directly.

Network based on something your prospect has mentioned. Maybe they're hosting a fundraiser you can help with, or maybe you can introduce them to people who are working on the same cause.

Here are a few other ways to catch their eye:

- 10 ideas to improve their product based on customer feedback
- Podcast or book recommendation that covers

an issue they're having

- Do they cook? I just had an X chat about pizza with one of my prospects

Maybe they're implementing a solution, and you've supported others doing the same thing. Connect those jokers and let them talk.

Years ago, Starbucks implemented a Tech Café for walk-up support on devices. Expedia was doing something similar, Tech Concierge, so I connected the two directors.

Just last year, Epic Games was looking to implement a vendor management system. Activision had just done the same thing, so I connected the two leaders and let them talk shop. Value to the customer, partnership from you— just one email connecting people added more value than any of the solutions I could have sold them.

Plus, I helped them avoid speed dating for business. The likelihood of them reading my next note just went up.

How Else Can You Catch Their Attention?

Eleanor Roosevelt is credited with saying, "Great minds discuss ideas; average minds discuss events; small minds discuss people."

If you want to meet with Elon Musk, try to connect with him on one of three levels:

- People – I'm friends with Johnny, and you're friends with Johnny, so we should be friends.
- Events – I'm interested in SpaceX launches, and you're interested in SpaceX launches, so

we should be friends and talk about SpaceX launches.

- Ideas – I believe Dogecoin is the future of interplanetary currency, and I have a few ways that could work at scale. Attached is a prototype. I'd like to work on this with you if you're interested.

Ideas are the strongest but also the hardest. Ideally, you have all three legs of the stool, but use what you have.

Before you get all bent out of shape because people aren't getting back to you, let me say it again: nobody cares about you. I know that hurts, but even your mom will miss a few emails, and you literally lived inside of her. Prospects need clarity on how you can help them. People are busy. Don't take it personally—they just didn't get to your amazingly well-crafted message. Assume thousands of unread notifications. Inbox zero is dead. Your note is in there somewhere and may never get discovered, and that's okay.

Connect based on people, events, and ideas. Eventually, if they're the right audience, you'll catch their attention.

The next question is an important one. What if they do open it? How do we craft something the prospect will act on?

WHY ARE YOU REACHING OUT?

You've identified the people you want to connect with. You've taken notes on their profile, and you understand some key things that might resonate with them.

Now take a quick breather and run through the scenario in your head.

At some point, a few of these prospects will ask you a simple question that many people trip on.

Why are you reaching out? What's the reason for your note, your email, your direct message?

It was my mother's response to all solicitors. It's a trick question, though.

Most people will respond with their objective. Their reason. To tell Mom about the product or service. To get her interest and close a deal or schedule a follow-up.

Something like this:

"Thanks so much for your time. I know you're busy, so I'll make this brief. Have you ever had costly repairs around the home? They sure don't build them like they used to. I've been working in the Northwest for thirty-three years ..."

And they'll go on like that for quite some time. A monologue. A one-sided conversation, and they've picked the wrong side.

The better answer is a reason she should take the call or read the email. A reason she shouldn't push delete, slam the door, hang up, or dump the letter in the recycle bin immediately. A reason that resonates with her.

What she needed to understand was how they could help.

"My company helps customers save time and money on unnecessary rip-and-replace repairs on their home through timely proactive maintenance."

What she needed to hear was specific.

"I was doing work at your neighbor's house last week, the Johnsons', and I noticed your deck needs some maintenance. I do that kind of work, and it'll save you money in the long run because you won't need to replace the lumber for another five years."

What she needed to hear was why she can trust you. Social proof.

"Anyhow, you can go ask the Johnsons about the work I did for them. It turned out great, they're happy, and it's guaranteed for the next twelve months."

And what she needed to hear was an easy onramp to working with you and some value being offered.

"I can set some time to meet next week after you have a chance to think it over. I'll already be in the neighborhood, at the Johnsons' doing their first month's check-in. I'll give you a free quote and project plan, so you'll know exactly what needs to be done even if you don't select me for the work."

The buyer's job isn't to download your capabilities and match them against their needs. That work is yours alone. That is the job, matching needs and wants with capabilities, and helping people understand why they should pick you.

If I were you, I would double-check my work before starting to push send. Are you being clear as to how you can help? Are you giving them specifics and not relying on them to connect the dots based on your laundry list of offerings?

- How you can help
- Specific capabilities match
- Social proof
- Minimal risk with onramps for the relationship

If you can check those boxes when you communicate with prospects, you'll help them make real progress, and you'll make progress too.

Before you engage, ask yourself the same questions, and make sure you've got great answers that put the customer's needs first.

Why are you reaching out?

POSITIONING

Congratulations. You've started to warm up some leads, and your network is growing. The world feels a little less cold, so you want to start reaching out to people directly.

Hold on for one more minute.

You won't succeed if you can't connect product and prospect. Value with the target. People need to be able to easily understand what your product is, what your service does, why your charity is special, and why an investment will matter to them.

The last step I need you to focus on before you reach out is positioning. Just like on the football field, if you play the same position as someone else, you've got a competition on your hands.

In business, you'd like to limit competition. As Peter Thiel would say, "Competition is for losers." And as I would say, proper positioning prevents piss-poor performance.

Positioning is the place a brand occupies in the mind of the customer, how it's distinguished from the products or services of its competitors.

No matter how great you are, if you go head-to-head,

you're going to have a collision. It's better to avoid all of that by being different. And if we can be different in a way that's useful to our customers, we can win the day.

Think through that customer journey before you start passing notes.

Positioning requires you to see the customer's point of view on the problem you solve, and the alternative ways of solving that problem. If you sell standard push lawn mowers, the alternative is getting yard service, or one of those new robo-mowers.

Positioning assesses the ways you're unique from those alternatives and why that's meaningful for customers. The gas mower is cheaper, but it takes time. To sell them, you need customers who are watching their budget and have Saturday free to work in the yard.

Positioning assesses the characteristics of a prospect who really values what you can uniquely deliver. We've narrowed our customer base to the homeowners who are on a budget and have Saturdays free. What else do they like about our offer? Easy: a best-in-class warranty, the quietest motor in the industry, and the most powerful mulch setting in its class, so they don't need to bag the grass.

Positioning understands the best market for your product, making your unique value obvious to your ideal customers. Based on everything we've learned above, we need to get these machines into Home Depot and Lowe's to find the do-it-yourself crowd. And we should enter markets with a long grass-growing season where these attributes are especially desirable.

The numbers game isn't going to work on its own. More volume, more budget, more amplification isn't enough. It doesn't help to be clear and loud if the other person doesn't speak the same language.

Make sure you're speaking their language, and get clear on your position in the market.

Otherwise, notes will be passed, and notes will fall short of their audience.

The good news is you've done most of the work already. You understand your customers, have a clue about their needs, and have been thinking about your product or service for quite some time.

This work isn't about creating the world's largest list of prospects. You want to find the few people who have the power and the knowledge to decide, in a market that needs you. That is going to be your niche in the great wide ocean of commerce. Some people just want the yard service, some want the robo-mower, and that's okay.

Don't try to be everything to everybody.

Take the time, trust your homework, understand your unique position, and only then will you be ready to start making direct contact with those prospects.

Speaking of making contact, I think it's time we started crafting our message.

CHAPTER FOUR: CRAFTING

"E-mail is like food. Good recipes produce good results, but you need to follow the proper steps."

– TIM FERRISS

THE CHALLENGE

In the early 2000s, Princeton University students who were enrolled in High-Tech Entrepreneurship got an up-and-coming Tim Ferriss as a guest lecturer.[12]

Tim didn't want to talk about technology stacks or digital transformation; he wanted the students to do something outside their comfort zone.

The challenge was to "contact high-profile celebrities and CEOs and get their answers to questions they have always wanted to ask." He even provided some extra incentive with a round-trip ticket anywhere in the world for the student who could contact the most hard-to-reach name with the most interesting question.

Ferriss' list at the time included Rick Rubin, Jeff Corwin, Francis Ford Coppola, and Jamiroquai.

The students received responses from the likes of George Bush and the CEOs of Disney, Comcast, Google, and HP.

How did they do it?

Ferriss says, "I do what I always do: find a personal e-mail, if possible, often through their little-known personal blogs, send a two-to-three paragraph e-mail that explains that you're familiar with their work, and ask one simple-to-answer but thought-provoking question in that e-mail related to their work or life philosophies. The goal is to start a dialogue, so they take the time to answer future e-mails—not to ask for help. That can only come after at least three or four genuine e-mail exchanges."

One student, Ryan Marrinan, applied the technique to connect with venture capitalist Randy Komisar.

His first e-mail mentioned reading Komisar's *Harvard Business Review* article "Goodbye Career, Hello Success,"[13] and asking him, "When were you happiest in your life?" Komisar emailed back with references to Tibetan Buddhism.

Marrinan's response was on point: "Just as words are inadequate to explain true happiness, so too are words inadequate to express my thanks." He also included his personal translation of a French poem by Taisen Deshimaru, the former European head of Soto Zen. An e-mail relationship was established, and Komisar even emailed Marrinan a few days later with a link to a *New York Times* article on happiness.

Keep in mind that Marrinan did a wonderful job using Ferriss' technique, but it was informed before he started. He didn't simply guess that happiness, Soto Zen, and poetry would resonate with the Silicon Valley VC; he did his homework and found uncommon commonalities. Komisar had recently published a book called *The Monk and the Riddle*, giving Marrinan even more information. Marrinan then crafted a great email that found its audience.

How can you craft a similar email? That's what we'll discuss next.

AIDA

This is what you've been waiting for.

In this section, the longest of the book, we'll walk through the real meat of *Passing Notes to Strangers*. Crafting your message.

There are several frameworks for this, but the tried-and-true method is AIDA. You might recall AIDA from the opening chapter, using the framework to pass notes in school, but it has been around for a long time.

In 1898, an advertising man named Elias St. Elmo Lewis wrote an article for *The Inland Printer* outlining the three advertising principles he had found useful throughout his career.

Lewis said, "The mission of an advertisement is to attract a reader, so that he will look at the advertisement and start to read it; then to interest him, so that he will continue to read it; then to convince him, so that when he has read it he will believe it. If an advertisement contains these three qualities of success, it is a successful advertisement."[14]

This process of getting a reader to continue through your advertisement, copywriting, or presentation is called the "slippery slope." When done well, it can be mesmerizing. I've caught myself 2,000 words deep on emails from The Motley Fool, a provider of stock tips, before finally snapping out of it and investing my money in an index fund.

Attract attention, generate interest, create conviction. It sounds familiar.

Over one hundred years later, Lewis' formula is mostly intact. It still works, and it's been refined into the acronym AIDA. AIDA is used in advertising, marketing, sales, copywriting, or just getting the neighbor to take their trash cans in from the curb.

AIDA represents the primary stages you'll need to navigate on a customer's journey. Not necessarily their buying journey—we'll get to that later—but their journey of awareness.

Alec Baldwin increased the public awareness of AIDA with his iconic performance in *Glengarry Glen Ross*.

That said, a better example of AIDA in action comes from the movie adaptation of Stephen King's *Rita Hayworth and The Shawshank Redemption*.[15]

Andy's Aida:

Andy Dufresne, the smart wife-killing banker, was also quite a salesperson. In this scene, he executes a near-perfect AIDA on the hard-nosed prison guard, Mr. Hadley.

Attention:

"Mr. Hadley, do you trust your wife? What I mean is, do you think she would go behind your back? Try to hamstring you?"

Interest:

"Because if you do trust her there is no reason you can't keep that thirty-five thousand. Thirty-five thousand. All of it. Every penny."

Desire:

"If you want to keep that money, give it to your wife. The IRS allows a one-time-only gift to your spouse for up to sixty thousand dollars. Tax-free. IRS can't touch one cent. It's perfectly legal. Go ask the IRS. They'll say the same thing. Actually, I feel stupid telling you this. I'm sure you would have investigated the matter yourself."

Action:

"But you do need someone to set up the tax-free gift for you. And that will cost you. A lawyer, for example. I suppose I could set it up for ya. That would save you some money. If you get the forms, I'll prepare them for you. Nearly free of charge. I'd only ask, three beers a piece for each of my coworkers."

Beautiful execution by Andy on the plate factory roof.

Now let's look at each stage of the AIDA framework in more detail.

ATTENTION

"Let's start at the very beginning, a very good place to start."

— SISTER MARIA (JULIE ANDREWS), THE SOUND OF
MUSIC

SUBJECT LINES

Let's look at Attention in more detail.

Attention can come in several ways, but it's critical in getting your audience to read the note you've put all this effort into. Don't gloss over this step. The reason to read on can seem obvious to you. You're selling a product you love, raising money for a charity that's important to you, or starting a business around your life's work. But to get someone's attention, you need to have empathy and understand what it's like to walk in their shoes. Understand why this is going to be interesting, helpful, or profitable for them.

And getting this across to your target starts right up at the top. If you're sending an email, that's the subject line.

People are more likely to read emails with subject lines that create curiosity or provide utility.

When we pass notes to strangers, we don't need to use the format we learned in English. Attention starts early, maybe even before they open the note.

Gary Halbert would start to gather his target's attention before they opened his letters.[16] He would make the outside look personal, handwritten instead of printed. If he was selling real estate, he'd put dirt or sand in the package, so when they felt the envelope, they'd be intrigued.

What's in there?

What you write in the body of your note means nothing if the target never reads it. Spend some time to make sure you'll catch their attention early.

For email, that's the subject line and the sender's name and address.

If you send your email from Spammer@Spambot.com, they might come to the crazy conclusion that it's spam. If your subject is "45-minute PowerPoint presentation about a software solution you don't really need," it's going to be tough for them to check the "Yes" box.

If every little detail gushes out before you get their attention, you're pitching them too early. Attention first.

They're more likely to give you some attention if you're familiar. If you've nudged them on social media as "Dave," and now you send them an email from "Dave," that's going to help. If the subject line is personalized, like "Note about your AI blog post," that might be enough to get the ball rolling.

Your attention grabber can't be just anything. It needs to be relevant to gain their trust. You can't yell "Fire!" in a crowded theater so you can sell them buttered popcorn as they head for the door.

The busier they are, the more utility you need to provide. They may not have time to get intrigued by some clever subject line; sometimes they just need the facts. Work to build curiosity and show utility.[17]

Here are a few examples I stole, so you can steal them

as well:

- Curiosity – "Appreciate your help yesterday," "Your blog post helped me lose 35 pounds," or "I couldn't think of anything creative, so I sent this instead"
- Utility – "Using your Chrome plugin to support homeless shelters [a case study]" or "Easy fix for the ecommerce issue you posted about"
- Both – "1 million hours available, just need a philanthropy to support" or "7 small upgrades for next year's conference (and 1 big one)"

If I were you, I'd make sure I incorporated the first thing they see into the attention section of my AIDA framework. Leverage utility and curiosity to keep them reading.

For email, that means adjusting your technique and incorporating it into the subject line, address, and even the preview.

For physical mail, make sure it looks like it could be from a friend.

For DMs, target based on their posts, their contributions on the platform.

WRITE MUSIC

People love short sentences. They love spaces between paragraphs. Part of your job is to make reading easy. Getting someone to pay attention to your notes is hard enough. You'd hate for them to get started but stop before the end because you made it hard on them.

Make it short, clear, and rhythmic.

"Easy books contain lots of short paragraphs," Stephen King discusses in his memoir *On Writing*. "Including dialogue paragraphs which may only be a word or two long—and lots of white space. They're as airy as Dairy Queen ice cream cones."

What is it about this style that works?

Part of it is progress. Readers love page-turners, right? So let them turn some pages. They'll go to bed that night with a feeling of accomplishment.

And with that accomplishment comes the sunk cost fallacy. They won't want to quit reading if they've already put time and effort in, so they'll continue.

Same with passing notes.

Whether it's a post, a DM, or an email, once they start

scrolling, they're more likely to keep scrolling. Otherwise, they must admit to themselves that their eight minutes reading this stupid thread was a total waste of time!

If I were you, I'd take my drafts and chop them up. Space them out. And make sure I'd exchanged all the ten-dollar words for fifty cent pieces.

Now let's talk a bit more about rhythm.

I don't know if I can make it clearer than Gary Provost has in his book *100 Ways to Improve Your Writing*.

He calls it writing music. Highlighting the importance of changing sentence length to give your reader's ears and eyes a break and grab their attention.

Attention? Yes. That's exactly what we're looking for.

Here is Provost's example:

"This sentence has five words. Here are five more words. Five-word sentences are fine. But several together become monotonous. Listen to what is happening. The writing is getting boring. The sound of it drones. It's like a stuck record. The ear demands some variety.

Now listen. I vary the sentence length, and I create music. Music. The writing sings. It has a pleasant rhythm, a lilt, a harmony. I use short sentences. And I use sentences of medium length. And sometimes when I am certain the reader is rested, I will engage him with a sentence of considerable length, a sentence that burns with energy and builds with all the impetus of a crescendo, the roll of the drums, the crash of the cymbals —sounds that say listen to this, it is important.

So write with a combination of short, medium, and long sentences. Create a sound that pleases the reader's ear. Don't just write words. Write music."[18]

This technique makes your writing more human, more readable, and it makes it more fun. Try it out. Your audience will thank you with their attention.

THE BYSTANDER EFFECT

"Billy, Billy, are you okay? Are you alright?"

Mr. Montgomery was going through the steps one more time before testing us. CPR certification was a mandatory part of ninth grade health class, and something I should have paid more attention to.

"You, David." He was pointing to me, David. "Go call 9-1-1."

This was important to him. Apparently, when you're in a group with an emergency, you don't just scream, "Somebody call 9-1-1!" You tell a specific person to do it. In this fictional training scenario, that person was me.

Why?

In 1964, Kitty Genovese was murdered outside her apartment in New York City. Thirty-seven neighbors saw the attack, and a few tried to call the police, but none of them came to help.

But why?

Picture yourself in a crowded restaurant when a rather

plump gentleman across the way starts coughing. A lot. Maybe choking. You think maybe you should see if he needs help, you think maybe he needs the Heimlich maneuver, but instead you keep chatting and enjoying your cheesecake.

What's happening here?

The bystander effect says that the greater the number of bystanders, the less likely it is any one of them will help a person in need.[19] It could be a bully, an assault, or someone drowning; people are more likely to help if there are fewer people there rather than more.

It's counterintuitive, but people assume someone else will do it.

Social pressures are at play. Bystanders are afraid they'll jump to the wrong conclusions. A man is talking to a little girl, and she's crying. *Is it his daughter? Is he a kidnapper? Can't go call the police every time someone's daughter cries. Shoot, my daughter was crying last night because she dropped a bag of Cheez-Its. The police showing up would have been a bit much.*

Herd mentality has an impact as well. Bystanders look around, nobody else is doing anything, they all look like nice, respectable people, so they figure nothing is really wrong. Meanwhile, everyone else is doing the same thing. Their collective inner monologues say, *Nobody else is doing anything. Maybe nothing is wrong*, so nothing happens, and the plump gentleman chokes on his bratwurst.

How does this affect you when passing notes to strangers?

If the recipient feels that they're just one among many to get the offer, they'll be less likely to read and respond.

It's the virtual equivalent of being in a large crowd.

In *Star Wars: A New Hope*, Princess Leia's urgent message was, "Help me, Obi-Wan Kenobi. You're my only hope!" and she included schematics to the Death Star. That is very specific, and it's not bad on the utility either.

Much more powerful than, "Can anyone in this galaxy help me out against the evil Lord Vader? Like, pretty please. Maybe give me a call and we can spitball some ideas?"

If I were you, I would make sure to do my homework. While I did that, I would highlight and double underline anything that would make the recipient feel like the only person in the room. Add something to your note that's the equivalent of "David, go call 9-1-1" or "Help me, Obi-Wan Kenobi. You're my only hope!"

INTEREST

"You can make more friends in two months by becoming interested in other people than you can in two years by trying to get other people interested in you."

– DALE CARNEGIE

BE INTERESTING

If you're following along with the AIDA framework, you'll see that the next step, after getting the attention of our prospect, is to build some interest.

Sounds easy enough, right?

The best way to build interest is to be interesting.

What do people find interesting? That's right, themselves. Building interest is always about relating what you do back to the customer.

You could use some interesting facts. If you have a new and growing company, maybe you could mention your growth rate, how many customers you have, or what clients you've signed. For those facts to make an impact, you'll want to choose information that's related to your audience and informed by your collecting. What industry are they in, what issues are they facing?

Facts can be interesting, but if they're off target, you'll sound like the kid from *Jerry Maguire*.

"Did you know the human head weighs eight pounds?"

Interest can be gained in several other ways, including

stories, humor, and questions. You can also be indirect, and use the classic headhunter tactic, "Do you know anyone else who is interested in this amazing, wonderful, life-changing product or service?"

Don't rely on a single tactic. Variety is the spice of life, and you never know what flavor is going to resonate with your audience.

If it's interesting to you, and interesting to other people you've met with, it might be interesting to the next person as well. Just make sure to keep the focus on your current prospect, keep things simple, and don't overcomplicate your messaging.

Complexity impacts readability, which is a key trait of great notes, and it's what we'll discuss next.

THE
PSEUDOSCIENCE
OF READABILITY

We pass notes to strangers to express an idea. Clearly sharing a vision for the future, a vision we hope the recipient will share. The best way to do that and get your point across to them is to keep it simple.

Don't muck it up by trying to use unnecessary, complicated, over-the-top words.

Notice I didn't say gratuitous, convoluted, extravagant vocabulary?

When you use the thesaurus, work your way down to simplistic words, not the other way around.

What you're trying to do with your writing is cast a spell over your reader, a spell that keeps them reading, and you don't want to do anything silly that'll break that spell halfway through. Grammar and punctuation can break the spell just like obscure and difficult words. Anything that trips up your audience and breaks their flow is a no-no.

This can be difficult. Mostly for your ego. You spent a lot of time in high school trying to learn these words so you could regurgitate them on your SATs. Congratulations. Now please don't take that Princeton Review angst out on the rest of us.

Here's what we know.

Readability scoring will identify a grade level associated with your writing. Flesch–Kincaid and Dale–Chall are two of the most popular formulas. Online tools are abundant, and your word processing program probably has these built into them.

The book in your hands is measuring as a 77 on the Flesch–Kincaid scale, which maps to the seventh grade, categorized as "Fairly easy to read." You're welcome.

The primary drivers are sentence length and word length. Sentence length is judged by the average number of words in each sentence. Word length is calculated by the average number of syllables in each word.[20]

In this writer's opinion, the science of readability is more like a pseudoscience.

Many people say Hemingway wrote at the fourth-grade level. He uses short words and short sentences, so some of these tools will agree. I'm not convinced. I read *The Old Man and the Sea* at sixteen and had no clue what it was about. And I still don't. Ask a fourth grader from your neighborhood to give it a read, and see what happens to your house this Halloween. *Trick or treat!*

Most people will recommend you target an eighth-grade reading level for a general audience. Think *Harry Potter* and *Jurassic Park*, not *A Brief History of Time*.

Studies have been done with newspapers and online writing. What those studies will tell you is that even a slight decrease in grade level, going from tenth grade to eighth grade for example, will increase reader numbers.

For emails, it'll increase response rates. People are more likely to finish reading your terrific AIDA formatted message if they can, in fact, read the message.

It makes sense. The lower the grade level, the wider the audience. But take it with a grain of salt. Many of the studies were done in the 1940s, when half of the US population didn't make it past the eighth grade. It's no wonder they recommend targeting a middle school level for material you want to be widely read. Today, 92 percent of the US population graduates from high school.[21]

In the 1940s, only 5 percent of the US population earned a bachelor's degree.

Today, roughly 40 percent of the US population earns a bachelor's degree.

So, what do we make of this? Do we need to dumb down our writing when 92 percent of people are at the twelfth-grade level or beyond?

First, we can aim a little higher and still reach our audience. Things have changed, and what is impacting today's writer has less to do with words per sentence or syllables per word and more to do with catching our audience's attention and keeping it in a world full of distractions.

How do you get them to start reading, and keep reading, with their limited time and attention?

Use the AIDA framework, edit the unnecessary out,

utilize format to increase readability, and know your audience.

Second, you should still use the screening tools to double-check your writing and make sure it's at the appropriate level, and then think about subtracting one or two grade levels. In other words, come in just a little lower than the education level of your target audience. That'll make it easy enough to read quickly and entertaining enough to keep them engaged

If you're writing for an audience full of MBAs, write at a college level. Maybe use some graphs, pie charts, or a lovely 2x2 matrix. MBAs love that stuff.

If they're PhDs, you can up that just a little more, but try to make the language palatable for them. A data scientist may appreciate more statistics. An author may value more colorful language. But we don't want to use a one-size-fits-all approach of writing everything at the middle school level.

TELL A STORY

Venture capitalist Chris Sacca has a saying: "Good stories always beat good spreadsheets."[22] One of the strongest ways to build up interest is through a powerful story. Stories are sticky. If done right, they're easily repeatable, so they can spread. And inside of a story you can sprinkle in all sorts of details that'll resonate with your audience.

I don't know many people who are experts on supply chain and manufacturing, but everyone has heard about Henry Ford and his use of the assembly line for producing cars. That is a remarkable story of transformation.

Likewise, many people know that Jeff Bezos started Amazon in his garage, and they might have heard the anecdote about increasing shipments by 100 percent. How did he do it? Instead of having his people on their hands and knees packing boxes, he got everything onto tables.[23]

If I were you, I'd find a few great stories in my industry. I'd get good at telling them. And just when things got better in the story, I'd insert my customer into the narrative.

For example, if you'd like to borrow Amazon's story to

highlight the way small changes make a big impact, you'd want to bring your audience into the story just when the shipments improve by 100 percent. You'd bring them in by suggesting they might have similar unlocks hiding in plain sight, just like Jeff did at Amazon.

One of the best things about a good story is that once someone hears the beginning, they're going to want to finish. They'll want to see how it ends. That's a powerful mechanism if you're trying to sell products, services, or ideas.

When we tell a good story, we create a slippery slope, getting our reader to "slide" from one part of our note to the next.

Telling a great customer story can take you through attention, interest, desire, and action. Most often this'll come in the form of a transformation story, the Hero's Journey.

You start out telling them that [Nike, Home Depot, Apple] started out just like them. Attention!

They had issues with [Issue #1] & [Issue #2], so they signed up with your [Solution A] and turned those issues around quickly. They crushed it. Interest!

Sales went to [Large Number], margins went to [Excellent Percentage], and that same thing could happen here at Acme Corp. Desire!

All they did was sign up for an eighteen-month contract, and I've got the paperwork right here; just sign the line that's dotted. Action!

Keep it snappy, start as close to the end as you can, and remember the story isn't about how great you are at passing notes to strangers—it's about how you can solve the prospect's problem. It's not a ship's log, and it's not your bedtime journal. It's a story. It has a beginning and middle and an end. Tell it, relate it to their situation, and ask them to partner with you.

The End.

THE ULTIMATE WEAPON

Jerry Seinfeld says, "Being funny is one of the ultimate weapons a person can have in human society. It might even compete with being really good-looking." The ultimate weapon sounds good to me.

Victor Borge says, "Laughter is the shortest distance between two people." We detailed in the "Collecting" and "Connecting" chapters of this book that we want that distance to be as short as possible. When we're passing notes to strangers, we want to break down barriers as quickly as we can, and humor is a great way of doing that. It can be used at any stage in the AIDA framework, but most often it'll be used to gain the interest of our audience.

Being funny is hard, but having a sense of humor is easy. Everyone likes a good laugh. You don't need to write your own material like Jerry Seinfeld; just steal from the best.

Do you think your uncle Mike wrote all those one-liners he repeats *every* Thanksgiving? Not a chance. He just paid attention to what made him laugh and tucked those jokes away in his toolbox, breaking them out when the conversation died down.

What he was doing was using humor to break the tension, and it's a useful skill.

"Consider how the traditional burlesque show alternates strippers with comedians," writes Chuck Palahniuk, describing the importance of building up and breaking tension. "Sex builds tension. Laughter cuts it. Such a program will keep the audience happy by first arousing people, then exhausting them with the release of laughter. Likewise, girlie magazines are famous for their formula of mixing nude photos with raunchy cartoons. Once more, one element creates tension. The other lessens it."[24]

I'm not suggesting you start adding nude photos when passing notes to strangers. I'm focused on how to break the tension and bring people closer together. Passing notes naturally builds tension. You're asking for their time and attention. Whether it's for sales, fundraising, or for a job, it all builds tension as we work through the AIDA framework toward that closing action. And that's a good thing. Without tension, we're unlikely to move our audience to action. Some laughter, a bit of comic relief, is more than welcome.

Too much tension, and people will stop reading. Keep them engaged by breaking it up with some humor. Balance the tension, build it up, and then release it as you work to build rapport and eventually a relationship with this person.

You have a variety of ways to incorporate humor in the digital age of passing notes. YouTube shorts, GIFs, and links to stories can all be incorporated into your messaging.

Most of all, showing your audience that you have a sense of humor makes you a real person, not just someone who is asking for something. Chris Voss, a retired FBI negotiator and author of *Never Split the Difference*, says, "Humor and humanity are the best ways to break the ice and remove roadblocks."[25]

So, if I were you, I'd listen to Jerry, Victor, and Chris. Crack a joke or two, and see where it takes your outreach.

ELEVATOR QUESTIONS

Have you ever made a purchase in an elevator?
Me neither. But we hear so much hype about the elevator pitch.

You can try to compress your best idea into a ninety-second elevator ride, but there's a good chance you'll miss a few key details.

Coca-Cola can run a ninety-second ad during the Super Bowl and make quite an impression, but that's only realistic because they have a hundred years of brand history. How many people watching those ads are hearing about Coca-Cola for the first time?

Your business is probably a little different than selling cans of carbonated sugar water. The company you've been building, the services you offer, is probably going to be hard to describe in that short amount of time. Plus, people don't like PowerPoint presentations in confined spaces.

Just as I've never made a purchase in an elevator, I've

never made a meaningful purchase from a single email either. A one-click buy on a one-time email? Even a Nigerian prince can't pull that off.

Let's change our focus. Instead of an elevator pitch, let's use elevator questions. Something that'll pique their interest. A good question creates a curiosity gap. It creates a space between what they know and what they might like to know. It leads them to seek out further information to close the gap. A good question might get them to follow you off the elevator, and that's the real goal of gaining interest: to keep the conversation going.

The same question in written form might get the dialogue going. You can even answer them yourself. List common client concerns and well-thought-out answers; this frequently asked questions (FAQ) format is very popular and provides a lot of utility. If you've done your homework, you'll know what they're working on and struggling with before you press send. You probably have the answers to the test.

But ask the question anyway. It'll engage the reader, since they won't be able to help but answer in their own head as they read along, if for nothing else than to see if they're right.

If I were you, I'd work on a list of commonly asked questions that highlight just how great your initiative is. And I'd pose those questions, a few at a time, to the people you're reaching out to.

With the intention of gathering interest, not closing the deal. Not yet.

DO YOU KNOW ANYONE?

"Do you know anyone?"
Somewhat different from an elevator question, this question is asking for referrals. It is implicit communication, rather than explicit communication.

It's indirect and often comes with a wink and a smile because the person you're after is them.

Like walking into that same elevator and asking your fellow riders if they know anyone who might want a bag of money. It's an attention grabber, it gets their interest, and most people will raise their hand.

It's softer, though. It makes it easier for either side to walk away while signaling an openness to further communication.

For example, as opposed to approaching someone at the club and asking them to dance, you might ask if they *know anyone who would like to dance*.

Of course, the intent is clear: you'd like to dance. But because you're being indirect, the person you ask doesn't get defensive. You've just asked for their help.

We use this technique in the recruiting industry.

Oftentimes, skills will be in high demand, and that's when clients will reach out to a recruiting firm for help. The general thinking is that those recruitment firms, or headhunters, are more aggressive than internal human resources recruiters, and they'll be able to find candidates.

The truth is, they're often less aggressive. And they use this passive trick to spread the word about openings and get people interested. I've worked in technology consulting and recruitment for almost twenty years, and the best people are never looking for work. You call them anyway, and you just let them know a little bit about the role and see if they know anyone who might be interested. Either way, the intention is clear: would you be interested in this amazing role over your current less amazing role?

All the while giving them an easy and comfortable way to decline the offer.

Just like the offer to dance, they can say, "I'll let you know if I think of anyone" just as easily as they can say, "I love this song. Let's go."

Two things happen when you pose the question.

We've talked about social proof, and this scenario creates something similar, something I call social spoof. It's a spoof because it's not real. At least not yet.

What happens when you ask someone if they know anyone who might be interested in [INSERT TERRIFIC THING] is this: they start picturing the thing, and they start imagining telling their friends about the thing.

They don't want to tell their friend about some crummy job opportunity, so they're thinking of why someone might want the role, why it would be a great move. And then something magic happens. They swap themselves into that new role. In their imagination, they see it clearly, and guess what? They get a little jealous. They say, "Why would I pass this sweet opportunity to Johnny? I'd be great."

It works in more than just recruiting.

Do you know anyone who might want to invest in this SaaS company that's growing at 2,000 percent a year and just signed up Google and Microsoft?

That venture capitalist will think about it for about twelve seconds before picturing themselves and *their* investment growing by 2,000 percent. It might be another fourteen seconds before they ask to sign the paperwork.

If it's so good, such an opportunity that you'd tell your friend, maybe you'd want to try it.

A girl asks you if you know anyone who wants to dance, and your mind drifts forward twelve years. You can see your friend, the guy you set up for that slow song at the club, and he's getting married to her. He has this wonderful life. All because you wanted to sit on the sidelines until they played some Drake.

It's even worse if you see your friend getting excited about the idea. That mimetic desire kicks in and you start thinking, *Wow, they really want to dance with this girl. What am I missing?*[26]

So, if I were you, I'd experiment with asking my audience if they know anyone. It gets them working for you and uses a passive strategy to get them thinking about your product or service.

DESIRE

"Desire is a contract you make with yourself to be unhappy until you get what you want."

– NAVAL RAVIKANT

WANTS AND NEEDS

The third part of the AIDA framework is Desire.
Make them desire what you're selling, and they'll
be unhappy until they get it.[27] We can do this
constructively by providing the things they already want
and need.

Sounds almost too basic, but that's a big part of your
prospecting work. To find the people that are highly likely
to have interest in what you're doing.

As Gary Halbert says in *The Boron Letters*, "People don't
always put their money where their mouths are; but
they nearly always put out their money where their true
desires are."

What that means is we have a good data point to use
when deciphering someone's desires: money. And when
we look at their buying habits, we want to see three
things: recency, frequency, and unit of sale.

Have they done it recently? Do they do it often? And
when they do, how big do they go?

If that all aligns with what you're selling, funding, or
promoting, that's your customer.

Whales in Las Vegas get the penthouse and the steak dinner comped, but only if they've played recently, they visit regularly, and when they bet, they bet big.

The venture capitalists you want to fund your business? Have they invested recently? Do they have a track record of working with businesses like yours? Do they cut the size of the check you're looking for?

If so, it's going to be no problem to create desire—you just describe the benefits they'll see if they buy, invest, or donate.

Keep in mind that desire is an emotion. It's not always grounded in the truth. You can't win desire with data alone. When you describe the benefits, you'll need to strike a chord with them personally. It's not enough to tell them the product is growing quickly; you'll need to connect that data point to how it'll affect them. Paint that picture for them.

Instead of saying, "This product will improve quality," you want to say, "This product will get you back on the golf course again instead of being knee deep in customer issues."

When describing financial benefits, include how that'll change their life, not just their bank account.

If it saves them time, describe how much time, and what they could do with that time. Describe what it would take for them to learn all the skills your firm provides. Describe them buried under a pile of books and attending countless seminars trying to do it themselves.

Desire is about benefits, and it's also about our next topic: transformation.

TRANSFORMATION

Transformation is the deepest human desire.

It is the narrative behind everything from religion to retirement planning. From salvation to snake oil.

People take the Hero's Journey, the Eightfold Path, and then cheapen it and use it to make a buck.

Before and after. It's the best sales pitch on the planet.

People will pay to be changed. And people always want to be changed.

This is the basis for late night infomercials like P90X, all the way to enterprise software sales. If you can get people from where they are to where they want to be, you've got a chance.

No matter how large the company, they're all in the same business.

Transformation.

Accenture, Microsoft, and even Waste Management. They all offer transformation, before and after, just like Tony Horton and Tony Robbins.

It's a stop-the-struggle pitch, a subtract-suffering pitch, and it's a good one.

Although it's a bit cliché, feel–felt–found is a common technique for communicating this.

When your prospect informs you that they're not a buyer today, you simply say, "I understand how you **feel**, and I've had many customers who **felt** the same way, and what they **found** was, the [insert product/service/investment] was integral to their [insert transformation]."

This is why schools hype their famous alumni. The future looks bright with that Stanford MBA, doesn't it? Just ask alumnus and Nike founder Phil Knight. He wasn't even top of his class.

This is why infomercials lean on their "geek to freak" customers. You'd finally be happy if you had abs, wouldn't you?

Designers. Before and after.

Makeovers. Before and after.

Personal trainers, investment bankers, and landscapers. Before and after.

Client testimonials. Five-star reviews. Recommendations. They're all touting one thing.

Transformation.

Tell a story. Spin a yarn about someone just like them, going through exactly what they're going through. Articulate the "man in a hole,"[28] and how you got them out of that damn hole, once and for all.

The faster the better.

How fast? How much weight? How successful?

Well, that's where we shift from story to study. The best tool for getting into those details is the case study.

CASE STUDIES

A case study can increase your response rate significantly. Why? Because your prospect is reading about somebody just like them. They relate, they see themselves in the same situation, and they want what that other person has.

We talked about telling a story to gain interest. We talked about the power of transformation. We can continue this flow by bringing a few case studies to the audience's mind.

The Difference Between A Story And A Case Study:

A story is a narrative. It tells a sequence of events and has a beginning, middle, and end. It can be fiction or nonfiction, *Goldilocks and the Three Bears* or the JFK assassination. It can be used to entertain, inform, or persuade. Stories can be used to build rapport, connect emotionally, and demonstrate value.

A good story is relevant to the audience's interests, and it's told in a way that's engaging and memorable. It should also be credible and believable.

A case study is a more detailed document that describes how users solved a problem or achieved a goal. It typically includes some background, the challenge being faced, the solution implemented, and the results they achieved.

Case studies are used to provide social proof and demonstrate the effectiveness of a product or service. They can be used in a variety of ways, such as in pitches, proposals, and marketing materials.

The main difference between a story and a case study is the level of detail. A story is a general narrative, while a case study is an in-depth analysis of a specific situation.

Stories are often used to introduce a case study or provide context. Case studies, on the other hand, are often used to provide proof of concept and show value.

You still want the focus to be on benefits instead of features, but because your reader has become interested at this point, you get a little bigger share of their time and attention. With that, you can build desire by sprinkling in some details they'll be interested in.

Michael Lewis told the story with *Moneyball*; Bill James provided the case study with *The Bill James Baseball Abstract*.

Malcolm Gladwell told the story with *Outliers*; Anders Ericsson provided the case study with "The Role of Deliberate Practice in the Acquisition of Expert Performance."

See why we start with the story?

Let's Put It All Together:

PASSING NOTES TO STRANGERS

Think of a teacher who's looking for a job in a new city. She's just moved from Chicago to Seattle. To highlight her skills and the value she brings, our teacher sends her resume and cover letter to the district administration, explaining an issue she worked on in her previous school district. State testing scores were slipping because the new residents in the district were first-generation English speakers. Strong in math, very bright, just a bit behind in English.

As part of the collecting phase, she's already researched this new school district. She knows they have a similar demographic. Scores are on the decline, a massive influx of new residents from out of the country.

While stalking the administration on LinkedIn, she notices that the district lost the chair of their state testing committee.

Her story will resonate. She knows it. But she can't just tell a fun story with a happy ending; she needs to give them more.

In addition to the story about the improvements in Chicago, she decides to include a case study.

The teacher suggests that she would be able to come in and hit the ground running, and the district could expect scores to improve by 15 percent in year one and 30 percent in year two, on par with what she accomplished in Chicago. But we don't want the school district to think Chicago was a one-time occurrence. That would be a success story, but it wouldn't give confidence that this would work in Seattle. To address this, she includes the system they used, developed as a joint venture between the Harvard Psychology Department and the UC Berkeley School of Education, funded by

Microsoft research. The schools are freely sharing details of the program, data from other school districts, and professional certifications, which our teacher has already obtained.

That all sounds a bit more robust, right?

With the improved scores, it would put the Seattle school in the top quartile for the state. Other schools with that level of performance were rewarded with additional funding through the national grant program signed into law by the Obama Administration. That is quite a benefit.

A performance like this would also put this administrator in a position for accolades, promotions, and maybe even a certificate for their wall. Just like it did for the leadership back in Chicago.

That sounds like a pretty good case study to me.

Describe the benefits on multiple levels, statistically, emotionally, and financially.

How would it feel to see those test scores come in, Mrs. Administrator? What would those scores do for the school? For your career?

Hopefully you can see how powerful a good case study can be when used in the AIDA framework, but what else can we include in our notes to stoke desire?

RECIPROCITY

The concept of reciprocity involves the hard wiring of human psychology. We're more likely to respond positively to a request if we're given a gift first. We feel indebted.

Studies have shown that customers are more likely to make a purchase if they receive a gift first. Again, we turn to Robert Cialdini and his bestseller *Influence*, where he discusses a study showing a 42 percent increase in purchase likelihood when customers got a free piece of chocolate as they entered the store. You may have felt this firsthand if you've visited a See's Candy store or a Costco Wholesale. Both businesses are known for their free samples and seem to be faring quite well.

Many charities will send stickers and badges if you donate, but the savvy organizations will send that gift before the donation. St. Jude sends me return address labels along with their ask for a donation because they know I'll feel some amount of indebtedness to them for the gift and want to reciprocate.

That is what reciprocity is all about.

And you can use it when you're passing notes to

strangers.

Writer James Altucher is known for sending his "10 ideas a day" to people he wants to meet.

Years ago, when Amazon was getting their Kindle Direct Publishing (KDP) business off the ground, Altucher sent them a list: "10 Ideas for Amazon to Improve their Self-publishing division."[29]

They liked the list.

They flew him to Seattle, showed him around the operation, and let him in on what they were working on.

He got to meet everyone, got to be at the center of the publishing universe, and got to plant a seed.

Not every note to a stranger will lead to a sale or an investment, but if you do it right, you'll reach your audience and make an impact on them. And that's what Altucher did.

The gift doesn't need to be a big budget item. I get offers for Apple AirPods every day in exchange for a meeting, but I already have a pair, so that's not a valuable offer. Think about reciprocity in terms of value, not just cost.

Can you come up with ten ideas? I'm sure you can.

If I were you, I'd look for ways to give before I get. I'd try to provide some amount of value each time I reach out, and I'd try to build up a level of reciprocity with my audience. That way, when the time comes to make a request of them, you'll have a much higher likelihood of success.

Remember, the proper time to make a request is after you've seriously fueled their desire. So don't jump the gun. They need to be all hot and bothered before you move on to the next step. Once you've properly primed the pump, got them wanting what you've got to offer, you can move along to the last step in the AIDA framework.

Action.

ACTION

"What's 'easy to do' is easy not to do."

– JIM ROHN

SIMPLE, SPECIFIC, SAFE, AND SMALL

Action is about pushing your reader to do something, anything, in addition to reading. They've made it to the end, and we want them to do more than move along to the next email.

A primary function of getting action is to make it simple. Like passing notes in class, yes or no works well.

You also want it to be specific. The last thing you want is for a willing participant to get confused about what next steps you'd like them to take. If they want to buy but are unsure how to do that, we've failed. If they're interested in investing but don't know how to get their money in, we've failed. If they'd like to hire you but don't know how to contact you, we've failed.

These are common blunders at the action stage of AIDA.

Simple and specific are typically handled with a simple ask and a time slot. "Can we meet? I'll be in your area on Tuesday. Would 10AM or 12PM work for you?"

Safety is the third aspect that's critical but often misunderstood.

Chris Voss, author of *Never Split the Difference*, discusses the two primal urges that drive everyone you meet: the need to feel safe and secure, and the need to feel in control. He says if you can satisfy these drivers, you'll be in the door with coworkers, clients, and everyone else.

The small ask is best here. If you try to close them via email on the first correspondence, they'll get defensive. What you'd like to shoot for with your early outreach is participation. You want them to read your message all the way through and act. Any kind of action will do.

Even negative outcomes can be helpful in getting your foot in the door.

Yes, you read that right. A negative response is much better than no response at all.

Number one, it gives the target a feeling of control, which we've discussed as a positive.

Number two, the fact that they responded is a form of compliance. You asked them to respond, and they did. Now you've got some dialogue you can build on. As part of a graduation technique, otherwise known as a "yes ladder," you can now reply with a larger ask, like why they chose not to sign up for the service, or if they use other similar products.

The goal of action is to get them to act. To get them to do anything related to the product. After all, action is the last part of the AIDA framework, and they must have read to that point for good reason. They must have some level of interest or desire.

Keep it Simple, Specific, Safe, and Small for the best

chance of getting your audience to act. And then build on that action.

GRATITUDE

It sounds basic, but it's often overlooked. Watch your tone, say please and thank you, and express gratitude.

These are things your grandmother called manners. They're the WD-40 we need when passing notes to strangers. Without them, your note has that annoying squeak.

To use another *grandmaism*, you catch more bees with honey than you do with vinegar. People are going to be more helpful if you make it an enjoyable experience. The alternative is pressure, guilt, and obligation. That may seem like the best course of action, but in the long term, nobody wants to have their arm twisted.

If you can express why this person should help you, you're nice about it, and they see some value, they might even be excited to help you. But nobody is excited to help if they're not appreciated.

Gratitude is a powerful force.

Adam Grant writes about an experiment he ran with his colleague Francesca Gino.[30] They asked volunteers to help students improve their cover letter for a job application. The students responded to the feedback with an acknowledgment, "I just wanted to let you know that I received your feedback on my cover letter," along with an added request for help on a second letter. Just 32 percent of the volunteers helped with the added letter. When the student used gratitude, adding, "Thank you so much! I am really grateful," the rate of helping on a second letter increased to 66 percent.

If I were you, I'd finish my notes with a nice cherry on top. Thank them for their time no matter what they decide to do with your offer or request. It'll improve your success now and in the future.

And it's just good manners.

AIDA COACHING SESSION

What follows is a quick coaching session I had with one of my teammates. It started like many of them do, with an instant message (cry for help?) that "Nobody gets back me!"

I asked the account manager—we'll call her Annie—to send some examples of what she'd been sending to prospects.

Here Are The Three Examples She Sent:

Hey Colin,

I appreciate you accepting my LinkedIn request! Hope you're enjoying the warm weather in Boston!

I just wanted to reach out because I know you worked with [Consulting Firm] in Seattle in the past and I just wanted to let you know that I'll be the new point of contact!

Do you have 10-15 minutes in the next couple of weeks to

do a quick introduction meeting?

Best,

Annie

* * *

Hey Matt,

Just wanted to follow up on my last message!

I'm [Consulting Firm's] new account manager supporting [Client Name]. We are a technology consulting firm and have worked with [Client Name] for 5+ years.

I would love to learn about your role and your team over either a cup of coffee or over teams. Do you have 10-15 mins in the next couple of weeks to chat?

Best,

Annie

* * *

Hi Susan!

I'm the new point of contact from [Consulting Firm], an approved supplier supporting [Client Name] with Consulting initiatives. I know it has been a challenging few weeks at [Client Business Group]. I'd love to learn more about you and your team! Are you available in the next few weeks to connect over coffee or lunch?

Looking forward to hearing from you soon!

Thanks,

Annie

* * *

What do you think?

What I'd like you to do is take out a pen and paper, or just mark things up in the margins, and go to work on these examples. Make the edits you think this account manager should make, or rewrite the whole thing.

Can you find the different AIDA components? What parts are missing?

Here Is The Email I Sent Back To Her With My Suggestions:

Annie –

I'm breaking out the red pencil on you here but don't feel bad and don't get overwhelmed. I'm super old and have been doing this for 20 years. The good news is that I can help you learn everything I know about cold outreach in just 10 minutes.

Call me if you want to run through some of this and brainstorm. I'm free until 4PM.

All three examples you sent lack a compelling reason for them to meet.

How will a meeting help them make progress with their work?

Remember that our priorities are different than theirs. Our #1 thing is meetings, activity, and projects but they have actual work to do. The only way they'll accept the meeting is if you can help them with their work, and it's unclear from your emails how we can do that.

Okay, how do we express our awesomeness to them?

Standard email should follow the same format as a sales pitch, which is the same format you'll see in marketing and copywriting and all sorts of other communications. The old school acronym is AIDA. Just like Glengarry Glen Ross which is a movie that is too old even for me but has one great scene[31] (don't click at work, don't click if you can't handle crass language, you've been warned, don't @ me):

Attention – Authentic, funny, cute, curious, direct

Interest – Endorsements, referrals, recommendations, data, quotes, story

Desire – Social proof, we've done x for y, and they got z (X = service they need, Y = Company they admire, Z = Outcome they covet)

Alec Baldwin has this D as "decision" and I think he is awesome but wrong.

Action -- Tell them what to do next, make it easy and safe.

Okay, breaking down your first email from below.

Attention: *"I appreciate you accepting my LinkedIn request! Hope you're enjoying the warm weather in Boston!"*

I like the "thanks for connecting," it shows you have properly stalked, but I do not like "enjoy the weather." It does not get any attention.

Interest: *"I just wanted to reach out because I know you worked with us in Seattle in the past."*

"Just" is a short but powerful word that you need to be careful with. It weakens your ask. Good to use when the ask is big like I "just" need to increase your bill rate

$500/hour. But it is bad on small items because it makes them even smaller. So small it's easily ignored.

"I know you worked with us in the past" is not all that interesting either unless it comes with an endorsement or something. Go farther.

Desire: *"I'll be the new point of contact!"*

The problem with this is now the message is delivered and if that is really what we are meeting about it falls under "that meeting could have been an email" category. They have no reason to meet. Okay, cool, you are the contact, and they can just reach out if/when they need something. This only works if we have current business that they will need to work with you on.

Action: *"Do you have 10-15 minutes in the next couple of weeks to do a quick introduction meeting?"*

This works. It's not super specific (i.e. Tuesday at 10AM) but it works. Good job.

Let's hold this up against the template from our team wiki. It's not perfect but it gets us a little closer. The more tailored and specific you can make this, the better.

Hey [Client],

Thanks for connecting on LinkedIn, it looks like you are working on [Project/Program/Initiative], and [Consulting Firm] has done several similar projects in [tech stack/industry/LOB]. You can find a bit more about that work [HERE/LINK]. [Consulting Firm] is currently working with [Line of Business 1 – 2 – 3], helping with one off consulting resources as well as managing larger outsourced programs. We partner with and help build teams across North America and Europe, including our two Nearshore Delivery Centers in Mexico. Can we set some time to discuss [Thing they posted about]? I'd be interested to hear about your work and share a few examples of where we've helped other teams make progress. Please let me know either way.

Best,

[Account Manager]

You don't need to follow any single template and the rules here are loose, but before you send you can easily ask yourself. Do I catch their attention, do I build interest and desire, and do I have a call to action?

Check those 4 boxes and push send.

Best,

Dave

* * *

What Did I Miss? What Else Would You Have Told Her?

Annie did give me a call, and we walked through some of the edits she was making, starting with Colin. She read her latest draft back to me and I had to ask, "Why are you reaching out to Colin?"

Annie said Colin was a referral from her brother-in-law who worked on the team.

"Your brother-in-law? A referral? Annie, don't bury the lead. That is the first thing you say: 'My name is Annie, and my brother-in-law James told me to reach out.' Why go into all this mumbo jumbo about technology consulting? You're reaching out because of a referral, and that's the strongest reach-out you can get."

I asked her to tell me more. Why did James think you should reach out?

She said, "That team does technology project work, and he knows that we helped them out with that in the past."

"What the... why is that not in the email? 'James told me to reach out. We've helped your team in the past.'" I asked her who we helped in the past? How did we help?

"Oh, we embedded some engineers with them for a short-term project."

I asked, "Who did we work on that project?"

"I don't know," she said.

"Okay, don't push send. Find that out. That's your social proof. You want to include that. It makes your email more compelling. It increases your chances of getting a response. Does this make sense?"

"Yes, that makes the email a lot better, thanks."

She read it back to me one more time, it was much stronger. We made a few adjustments as she went, helping the flow. Making it more musical.

"Yes, that's it," I said. "It's not perfect. They're never perfect. But it's good enough. And it's worthy of a response. Get those last few details and push send."

The Final Email:

Hey Colin,

I got your name from my brother-in-law, James. He

thought my consulting firm would be a valuable resource for your team to support future technology projects. Additionally, we've done a bit of work in your organization before, building analytics dashboards for the online services business.

From what James tells me, you are looking at different options to better utilize ServiceNow as a workflow solution. We just happen to be a certified partner for ServiceNow. I've included a link below to some of our project work and testimonials.

Can I put some time on your calendar to discuss your vision in a bit more detail? If it seems like a match, we can frame out the project and pull together a formal proposal.

Best,

Annie

What do you think? Better, right? It took a little time to build it out but the chances of getting a response went way up from the first outreach.

CONCLUSIONS FROM CRAFTING

Okay, we're done writing. How do you feel? That was a load of information, and it'll take a lot of practice to get good, but that's not the last step in passing notes to strangers.

We know our customers, we know how busy they are, and we know that even with the most conscientiously crafted notes we might not get a response. That can sting, but we can't just give up on them.

We care too much to let that happen.

The last part of passing notes is to do just that. Care.

Proper care is what's needed to sustain the momentum we've been working to build. That means you see things through with proper follow-up. It means you keep working on the prospect's behalf, even if they don't notice it quite yet.

So, before you start launching those custom notes and DMs, read on and find out the best ways to stay on top of all the work you've done and make the most of it.

CHAPTER FIVE: CARING

"In the short term, you are as good as your intensity. In the long term, you are only as good as your consistency."

– SHANE PARRISH

YOU'LL NEED TO CARE

You'll need to care, and that's harder than you might think. It cannot be faked.

It means you put in the time and effort, you follow up and add value, and you focus on quality and positive outcomes.

Most people don't follow up. In sales, it's called a "drive-by," where you spray calls, emails, or advertising "bullets" and drive off at top speed.

It doesn't work. You can't land a deal, investment, job, or date that way.

The first outreach might not land. And even if it does land, it often takes multiple touchpoints to get someone to act. Companies differ based on their clients and their services, but it's common for a prospect to have five to eight touch points before converting to a customer.

Show that you care by following up, showing your work, showing your progress, adding value, and staying relevant.

When it's all said and done, you'll create the *Idol effect*,[32] and your prospects will become customers and fans of what you do.

WHERE THE MAGIC HAPPENS

Follow-up is where the magic happens.

Follow-up feels low status, but it packs a punch.

Follow-up seems remedial, but it's what successful people do.

Remember your mom and your room? She was following up.

Remember your coach and your off-season training? That was a follow-up too.

But somehow if the boss does it, he's a micromanager. If the salesperson does it, she's pushy, or worse. Sometimes you don't follow up with prospects because you assume they don't want what you've got, they're passive, they just don't want to say no. They don't like you, and they don't like your ideas.

You feel like it's nagging. Pestering.

You assume the worst, and avoid the follow-up.

You talk yourself out of it.

Instead of assuming the worst, assume the obvious. They're busy. They forgot. They haven't gotten around to it yet.

You're offering value, right?

Maybe you didn't express the value well at first. This follow-up is your opportunity to express it better.

Maybe they forgot. This follow-up is your chance to remind them.

Maybe they missed the email altogether. This follow-up is your opportunity to reintroduce it.

All the reasons not to follow up have to do with what Steven Pressfield calls resistance.[33] This is the universal force that has one sole mission: to keep things as they are. Those assumptions you're dreaming up say more about you than them.

Those assumptions say you don't have confidence and conviction in what you're doing.

Those assumptions say you can't quite put your finger on the value.

And that's what we call a personal problem. Maybe some journaling will help you get over it. Just don't go pointing fingers at the boss or the prospect; instead, spend some time to reconnect with why you reached out in the first place. You do know the reason, don't you?

And if that reason still holds water, if the room still needs to be cleaned, the off-season training still needs to be prioritized, and the product still helps the customer, follow up on it.

Exactly how to follow up is what we'll discuss next.

THE YES LADDER

Do you have a big ask?
Start small, and follow up.

Need a job? Ask the company president for advice about their success. Cold email someone and tell them you admire them, you'd like to follow in their footsteps, and then ask how they would begin again if they were twenty-two years old.

These types of questions are not only flattering, but they're small and easy requests of high-powered people, and they'll start the dialogue with them.

What if you're trying to raise some money? Instead of immediately asking the big donor you don't know for cash, ask them how rich-powerful-awesome people decide what causes to give their money to.

Again, it's a smaller ask that gets the ball rolling and opens the lines of communication.

It also gives you the keys to the castle.

You can then shape the outreach to the way they assess their charitable contributions.

This is called the Foot in the Door Technique, or the

Yes Ladder.

Two Stanford researchers, Jonathan Freedman and Scott Fraser, set out to answer a question many of us have asked before.

How can a person be convinced to do something they would rather not do?[34]

One common way of attacking the problem is to exert as much pressure as possible on the reluctant individual. Force them to comply.

But what if there were another way?

The professors wanted to see if a small request was more likely to gain compliance with a larger demand. Commonly referred to as the foot-in-the-door technique and is reflected in the saying that if you "give them an inch, they'll take a mile."

It's also the engine behind many advertising campaigns that ask the consumer to do anything relating to the product involved, even sending back a card saying they don't want it.

The researchers conducted a field experiment. Housewives were asked to allow a survey team of five or six men to come into their homes for two hours to classify the household products they used.

That is a pretty big ask.

What they found was that making a smaller request first leads to better outcomes.

Only 2 percent of homeowners agreed to the in-home survey on first contact, but over 50 percent agreed when a prior call was made to them taking a shorter, over-the-phone survey on the same topic.

The basic idea was that once someone has agreed to any action, no matter how small, they tend to feel more involved.

The two researchers conducted a second experiment to verify their findings. They went door to door in a small neighborhood asking people to put signs outside of their home to "Drive Carefully." Only 20 percent of people said yes when asked to put up a large sign. However, researchers found that they could get 76 percent of the residents to say yes if they asked them to first put up a smaller three-inch sign.

Starting with a small request will help you get a "yes" on a bigger request later.

Have you ever told a friend you can't go out on a Friday night, and they convince you with "Just one drink. I'll buy"? Next thing you know, it's 2AM and you left your iPhone on the toilet three bars back.

When passing notes to strangers, your language matters, but so does the size and frequency of your request. Start with asking them to be friends on LinkedIn, then exchange emails. Allow for a few positive interactions before you make your way to the pitch deck.

If I were you, I'd start small and light, not large and dense.

DENSITY

Density is a concept that people often struggle with. "When should I follow up with them?"

It's a common question because there is no straightforward answer. It is going to depend on several variables. A good rule of thumb is to go with a lighter touch of higher quality, but some people just need a nudge, a reminder.

I get responses back all the time with a genuine "Thank you for following up. I really do want to meet, but the email got buried."

So, help them out.

Sometimes people don't follow up because they feel like they're being annoying. So, add value, make them smile, and make them feel a positive emotion. You risk being annoying but if you do it right, you'll move them forward.

You want to stay in their mind, you want to avoid the drive-by, so how often should you follow up?

I'll answer that question with a question. Does the timing have an impact on the recipient?

If you're hosting an event in July and want them to be a speaker, you need to know if they're willing before the schedule is released. This means timing has an impact, and a higher density is only practical.

If your seed round is closing and you want to know if they're interested in investing, that's also a time-bound conversation, and a higher density is reasonable.

What is more common, though, is urgency stemming from the salesperson or entrepreneur. Like the quarter ending with them just short of hitting their revenue target. They take out all that sales aggression on their potential customers, they use that timing to fuel their outreach, but the end of the quarter means nothing to the recipient. They can buy on the third of January just as easily as the thirtieth of December.

And treating your audience that way is really uncool. So, ask yourself, is this urgent for me or for them? Follow-up density depends on the urgency.

If it's not urgent, there are countless easy ways to stay relevant with them without being annoying. Here are a few.

Start Spreading The News:

I've built relationships over the course of months and years by simply following up when I've had some news to share. Nothing is scheduled, just sharing when something comes up.

I'd make a list of my prospects and put them in buckets for the type of buyer they were. If our company had a new data analytics solution, I'd share that with all the people in the data analytics bucket. Pretty basic stuff.

It could take several quarters, but the message was always different, never "Just following up for that coffee." And it added value. Eventually, they would see something that resonated, and they would have all our past correspondence in one single email thread for reference. That built enough trust to call for further action.

If nothing else, it showed I was conscientious enough to not get fired like the other sales reps.

So, ask yourself, do I have news to share?

Share Something Valuable:

Value is different from news. What we want to show them here is something that you think fills a need. Have they posted that they need to hire an engineer? Hook them up with your engineering friend. Did you notice that they moved overseas to the company HQ? Send them that podcast about the expats of Copenhagen. Did they just publish a book? Hype it for them and share the results.

There are too many ways to add value to list them all here. What I want to emphasize is that there are reasonable, *non-annoying* ways to reach out, increase your density, and grow the relationship before you have a relationship.

If I were you, I'd ask myself if there is a way to add value to my audience that doesn't add value to my bottom line. Their goals, not yours.

Show Progress:

What have you accomplished? What have you been

working on that might be interesting to them?

"I emailed you 5 years ago about speaking at my 300-person conference. I'm asking you again but this time it's different. It's now a 3000-person conference."

That is an email thread five years in the making. Sometimes progress takes time. And that's some great progress to report on. It shows that you're growing, and there might be a good reason, so maybe they should get with the program as well.

If I were you, I'd ask myself what progress I have made, and who might be interested in that progress?

If none of these are viable, if you don't have news or progress, if you can't add value and it's not urgent, just wait.

Take a beat and do some work. Make some progress. Follow up when you have something more compelling to put in front of them.

THE "I JUST" FOLLOW-UP

Have you given up on this?
Circling back.

Putting this back on your radar.

Bumping this thread.

Bubbling this up.

There are lots of cliché ways to follow up, and most of them, innocuous as they may be, simply don't work. What they all have in common is minimization and selfishness.

Which leads to my least favorite follow-up of them all.

The "I just" follow-up.

The most common is the valueless "I just wanted to follow up."

Seems like a reasonable opener, but it does two things that aren't helpful for you or your customer.

1. Starting with "I" makes the note about you rather than them. Pretty selfish, right?

2. Starting with "just" minimizes what you have to say next. It's a small but powerful word that makes whatever comes after seem like no big deal. So don't "just" yourself and your message if you feel that your note is important enough to read.

Find a way to start your note with something of value to them, something they want, or something they're interested in. Remember attention? That is needed every time you reach out, not just the first time.

Have a reason to follow up besides the follow-up. That should be easy because it's probably the same reason for your first outreach if they haven't responded, or it's the progress you've made on their request if they have responded.

But don't stop there.

Continue to add value.

"This article made me think of your blog post from the summer."

"Hey, did you see this [excellent, hilarious, helpful] video your CEO posted?"

"You mentioned on X that you had a big presentation coming up. Here is a great post by Seth Godin on how to make it a success."

The more thought you can put into your outreach, the better your open rates and conversion will be. The higher likelihood you'll have of landing the job or the investment.

It takes effort and caring, but it's worth the time.

And it can be recycled. If the link to the video gets a

response, do something similar for others.

If the advice on presentations resonates, store that for the next time.

You don't need to become a homesteader, growing each ingredient from seed, going farm to table on each piece of content. You simply want to spend some time to thoughtfully assemble the ingredients, so you can create terrific meals on any occasion.

THE IDOL EFFECT

The reason American Idol works is because people pick their winners early and stick with them. They tune in for the whole season, cheering and voting along the way, and telling their family, "You know, I really do have an ear for this stuff."

The audience becomes part of the journey. Shoot, even the great Carrie Underwood was up there clucking like a chicken to connect with fans during her first audition.[35]

Polish is not required.

The *Idol Effect* creates a two-sided relationship. It creates buy-in without any official partnership. It's something we all love to do on some level. Like your favorite audiophile telling you they've been listening to Coldplay since their first practice in the bathrooms of Ramsay Hall. It feels good to be early and right.

If you're the new kid, the new employee, you can leverage the *Idol Effect*.

Perfection is not required.

What is required is a spark, a connection, some personality, and some promise. Those potential partners, buyers, and investors, they want to relate to you.

Maybe you need some coaching. No problem, let your fans see your work. Let your coworkers in on your progress. Let them know what you've tried, what you think might work. The person pushing their car to the nearest service station is more likely to get help than the hitchhiker. If they see you working, people will jump in with you, get their hands on the back bumper, push, and contribute to your success.

Maybe you need to learn the business and refine your skills. Good. Make your clients aware of the time you're putting in. They'll see you grow and improve; they'll be cheering for you. They'll be getting themselves ready to buy, in the process.

If you really make an impression, they'll tell their friends.

Yes, they'll do it as a favor, but it'll also make them feel like an expert. Like they played a part in your success. People love to say "I knew it" almost as much as "I told you so."

But it won't happen without effort. People are more likely to help people who help themselves.

If I were you, I'd make it easy for them to become a fan. Show them a flash of what's to come, and pair that with some personality. Make small check-ins, and show your work so they can easily see how far you've come.

Make it easy for them to cheer you on and spread the word.

MIND THE GAP

No callback after the first date?
Must be bad breath, Bad conversation, Thinks I'm ugly, They heard a rumor about me. All this stuff runs through your head, and 99 percent is false.

When you leave a void in your story, the customer will think, *Dude is a slacker, Dude can't help, Dude is not interested in the work.*

If there's a gap in the story, they can't help but fill it in.

The world is full of the unexplained and the unexplainable, so we happily write the narrative, script the drama, and conjure the heroes and villains.

Let's not let the truth get in the way.

The bigger the void, the more ridiculous the claims. The bigger the gap, the more room for creativity and conspiracy. It's almost instantaneous. You see somebody walking down the street, through your neighborhood, and the backstory comes together immediately.

How did they get there?

"I bet their car broke down."

Reasonable, but not enough to satiate. Could they be a

runaway? Did they rob the neighbors?

"Bad home life in the Midwest, no doubt. They moved west, got strung out on smack, and now they're walking my streets on the hunt for our children. Save the children!"

Much better. We can work with that.

Some people do it for sport. It's called people watching. And it's not just my mom filling in the gaps for runaways and tramps. This is a natural human tendency; we all do it to some extent.

Yes, you do it as well.

In the same way our brain triangulates the landing spot when someone tosses us a frisbee, our brains are triangulating all the things around us.[36] They're working to predict outcomes at every turn.

When we leave a communication gap, we create misunderstandings. Miscalculations. What is really going on?

When we don't follow up, when we start some correspondence and then trail off, what do our prospects think?

Must be bad breath, Bad conversation, Thinks I'm ugly, They heard a rumor about me. All this stuff runs through your head, and 99 percent is false. But it doesn't matter what's true; it matters what they believe.

We need to mind the gap, stay aware of this human desire to predict. Control the narrative, communicate, and help our readers see the world more clearly. No prediction needed.

One terrific way to do that is the Don Vaughn Method.

145

THE DON VAUGHN
METHOD

Don Vaughn is a neuroscientist who works with David Eagleman at Stanford University.[37]

But his method isn't about neuroscience; it's about passing notes to strangers.

Eagleman is the author of *Sum: 40 Tales from the Afterlives*. It's a bestseller that has been translated into thirty-three languages and turned into two operas (by Brian Eno and Max Richter).

It's a good book, and like many good books, nobody wanted it.

Eagleman had collected a stack of rejection letters as high as the book.

People would write back and say, "Hey, I really liked this book, but I have no idea where I would put this in the bookshelf," or, "I don't even understand what this thing is."

They were confused.

That went on for a long time, and Eagleman was

certain that the book was never going to see the light of day.

And then finally, Eagleman came up with an idea. There was a particular literary agent that he wanted to speak with, so he figured out three different ways to reach out to her within forty-eight hours. She would be hearing from three different people in quick succession. No communication gap being left with her.

It worked, they talked, and she agreed. Two days later, they sold the book to a publisher. It had been a long, extended failure, but Eagleman just kept banging on that door until it finally opened.

What kept him going?

A series of events took place years before the book was written when Eagleman was working at the Salk Institute.

A high school class was visiting Salk during science day, and Eagleman gave a talk to the students, discussing his work. One of the kids came up afterward and said, "This is what I want to do. Can I work with you?"

Eagleman said, "Sure, write down your phone number on the dry-erase board."

The kid wrote it down and the next day, the dry erase board got erased. Eagleman was busy and simply forgot about the kid. But the kid didn't forget about Eagleman. He left him a voicemail saying, "Hey, I'm the kid."

Eagleman was impressed and thought, "Oh, I've got to call this kid back," and then got busy again and forgot. But the kid didn't forget about Eagleman and had his high school teacher write a letter saying, "Hey, this is just a letter to recommend that kid."

Then Eagleman got another call.

And another letter.

Eagleman wasn't annoyed. He wasn't put off. He was thinking, *Wait a minute. I don't want to miss this kid. This kid's amazing.* The kid ended up working in Eagleman's lab and for sixteen years has been his closest collaborator.

The kid's name is Don Vaughn. And what he did is called the Don Vaughn method.

The Don Vaughn method targets someone and reaches out to them from different angles in quick succession to make sure they don't forget.

Keep in mind, it's not spam; it's specific. Don was targeting David Eagleman. David was targeting a specific literary agent.

How can you use the Don Vaughn method?

Do your homework. Understand your customer. Meet them where they are, and provide them with what is useful and relevant.

Over a brief period, reach out to them in a variety of ways.

Like and comment on X, target on LinkedIn, have a reference send them an email, share or link back to their blog from yours, or get involved in the same charity.

You call in all the favors at once.

Don was omnichannel marketing himself, without the bells and whistles. And it worked.

He had Eagleman's permission, and he used it.

This can be done with varying levels of density. Don was heavy-handed, but you can have a lighter touch as well. A targeted advertisement followed by an email, followed by a call. It can almost feel like déjà vu for the audience. They'll ask themselves, "Where have I seen this name before?"

Eagleman was impressed because he was busy, and he couldn't remember to call Don back. So, when he was trying to get his book published, he thought, "I'm going to use the Don Vaughn method and hit this agent from every angle I can."

And it worked.

CONCLUSION

"Nothing will work unless you do."

– JOHN WOODEN

THE BAADER–MEINHOF PHENOMENON

One last bit of science for you before the book concludes. The Baader–Meinhof phenomenon.[38]

This is what's happening when you're shopping for a new car and start to see that car everywhere. It's also called the "frequency illusion," and it's just your brain becoming attuned to that information, making you more likely to notice it.

The same way your English teacher can look at your paper for seven seconds and find a bad piece of punctuation.

The same way the announcers on *Sunday Night Football* can see the slightest early move from the offensive line.

Their brains are so attuned to those things that they jump out at them.

And that's exactly what'll happen to you after reading

this book.

There is a great scene in the movie *Boiler Room* where Seth (Giovanni Ribisi) takes a cold call from the local newspaper salesman, Ron.

It's a Saturday morning. Seth is sitting at the kitchen table eating cereal.

Before Ron can even start his pitch, Seth tells him, "I'm not interested." Ron starts to give up and apologizes for the interruption, so Seth gives him a hard time, "That's your pitch? You consider that a sales call?"

He explains to Ron that someone from the paper calls every Saturday, and it's always the same lackluster attempt, so he urges Ron to try it again.

Ron dives in and gives Seth his most spirited pitch. He gathers some attention and gains a bit of interest. Seth is excited and says, "Alright, Ron. Now that was a sales call. Good job!" Ron moves to close with his call to action, "So, are you going to buy a subscription?" to which Seth replies, "No. I already get the *Times*," and hangs up.

I love that scene.

Seth has spent the whole movie learning about sales, about closing, and now he's seeing it clearly all around him. He is recognizing a good pitch versus a half-assed attempt.

I hope you'll do the same.

I hope you'll notice an email or a billboard or a call from the local newspaper for what it does well and where it falls flat. Does it catch your attention? Does it build interest and desire? And the part that's most often neglected, does it have a clear call to action?

I hope you'll see where an outreach is failing because of the bystander effect, and you'll find the strategic use of reciprocity.

If you're observant, all of this will inform your own outreach. You'll notice what works and why. You'll borrow ideas, steal strategies, and get better.

The best part: As you get better, the outcomes for your customers will get better as well. You'll waste less time. Your own time and theirs. And you'll do a better job of connecting what you offer to those it can help.

PASSING NOTES TO STRANGERS

Passing notes to strangers. How to write in a way that'll reach your people, when they don't know they're your people, is one of those simple-not-easy skills that makes the world go round.

It has many components, but it's mostly about providing value and building trust. It makes me think of a story Seth Godin tells about marketing.

"Take a ten-dollar bill to the bus station, then go up to someone and tell them, 'I'll sell you this ten-dollar bill for a buck.'

Nobody will buy it from you.

Why? Because people don't go to the bus station to make financial transactions. And people don't like dealing with insane people. And either you're insane, or it's not a real ten-dollar bill.

Or try it this way. Go to your neighbor's mailbox, drop off a ten-dollar bill, and run away. Then do it the next day and the next day, and on the fourth day knock on their door and say, 'Hey, I'm the guy who dropped off ten-dollar bills the last three days, and I'll give you another ten-dollar bill for a buck.'

Now they'll know you're insane, but insane in a very specific way, and they'll know you can be trusted. You've provided that value.

Before you leave, tell them you'll be in the cul-de-sac the next day giving ten-dollar bills for a buck and ask if they'll bring some friends."

The story stops there, but I'm willing to bet that a few deals were closed in the cul-de-sac that next day.

The story isn't about exchange rates, or ten-for-one deals. It's about value, reciprocity, trust, and service.

It's also about meeting customers where they go to buy instead of surprising them, ambushing them, putting them on a spot, twisting their arm, and coercing them. Knocking on their door or calling during dinner because you know they're home. Sweet-talking them into a meeting. That's not the path to a happy customer.

Where do people go to buy? They go online. Websites, social media, and email.

When I log into Instagram, I know that companies are going to pitch me. They're going to put something in front of me that I was talking about, searching for, or looking at. And I freely make that exchange as I walk into the virtual marketplace.

When I go to my email inbox, I know that a huge portion of those emails are pitching something. And even though I tell myself I don't need anything, that I'm not buying, I still open a handful. I still read a few.

What do I open? What do I click on?

Typically, they're messages from companies and people that do the following:

They know who I am, and they care who I am. They target me specifically based on what I buy or what I'm interested in.

They have my permission. They have offered some sort of value in the past, in exchange for permission to reach out in the future.

They're relevant. They do the homework and serve things I'm interested in. I'm not in the market for diapers. I'm not in the market for cigarettes either. They know that, and they don't spray and pray on my time.

They don't overwhelm. Companies that keep my permission to engage understand density and get it right.

That sounds a lot like collecting and connecting, crafting compelling and thoughtful correspondence, and caring with meaningful following up. Those are the basics.

It can get more complex. Figuring out where people buy and what they want is a business filled with psychology, science, and statistics. Tricks and tactics are abundant, but principles are few.

We can simplify, though. Passing notes to strangers is a skill we've been honing our whole lives.

Remember "Check yes or no."

I've tried to leave you with some of the principles.

I didn't know it at the time, but I started drafting this book over twenty years ago. Taking notes, noticing what worked, trying to understand and learning from rejection. When I finally got into leadership, one question was more common than all the others: "Why doesn't anyone get back to me?"

I'd review their audience, their targets, their prospects, and ask a simple question: "Why did you reach out to them?"

I'd review their outreach, I'd look for something to catch the attention of their reader, build interest and desire, and of course that clear call to action.

And when the target was right, and the message was clear, I'd look under the hood at their follow-up. A quick drive-by isn't going to get the job done.

Collect, connect, craft, and care.

But I mentioned a fifth C at the start of this book. Commit.

To steal a bit more from *The Shawshank Redemption*, "If you've come this far, maybe you're willing to come a little further." The ideas in this book take some commitment. They take more time, more thought, and more energy than the alternative. They also provide better outcomes, greater productivity, and more satisfaction.

Nobody wants to spend their working life analyzing open rates and trying to outsmart spam filters. Nobody wants to make their work about tricks, clickbait, and coercion.

The ideas in this book will allow you to spend your days in the support of a mission instead of being a mercenary.

These ideas work, but only if you do.

WIN WITH FLYNN

For more writing from David Flynn, please subscribe at www.winwithflynn.com to receive a weekly blog post as well as updates on future publications.

www.winwithflynn.com

ABOUT THE AUTHOR

David Flynn has twenty years of experience in business development, sales, marketing, and consulting. He is a graduate of Washington State University, where he studied business and writing. David started blogging at www.winwithflynn.com in 2022. Posts go up every Monday covering business, creativity, and personal development.

David lives in Sammamish, Washington, with his wife and two kids. He enjoys sports, business, and playing outdoors, as well as music, movies, reading, and cooking.

ACKNOWLEDGMENTS

I received two distinct reactions when I told people I was writing a book.

The first and most common? Total, painful indifference.

The second was genuine interest and support that was incredibly helpful and appreciated. The response that says, "Of course you are. You should absolutely be writing a book. Where can I buy twenty copies?"

For those who provided the second, I'd like to take a moment to say thank you here, in a format that will live with this piece of work wherever it may go.

Special thanks go to:

Liz Flynn, Patrick Flynn, and Kerry Lohr. For your encouragement, time, and attention.

ENDNOTES

[1] "How Things Fly," *National Air and Space Museum*, https://airandspace.si.edu/exhibitions/how-things-fly

[2] "How Fast does a rocket have to travel to get into space?," *Cool Cosmos*, https://coolcosmos.ipac.caltech.edu/ask/267-How-fast-does-a-rocket-have-to-travel-to-get-into-space-to travel to get into space?

[3] "Rick Rubin in Conversation with Malcolm Gladwell," *Broken Record Podcast*, https://www.pushkin.fm/podcasts/broken-record/rick-rubin-2

[4] Chouinard Y., *Let My People Go Surfing*, Penguin Books

[5] "Pareto principle," *Wikipedia*, https://en.wikipedia.org/wiki/Pareto_principle

[6] Halbert G., *The Boron Letters*

[7] Grant A., *Give and Take: Why Helping Other Drives Our Success*, Penguin Books

[8] Cialdini R., *Influence: The Psychology of Persuasion*, Harper Business

[9] Becher J., "Do Me A Favor So You'll Like Me," *Forbes*, https://www.forbes.com/sites/sap/2011/11/16/do-me-a-favor-so-youll-like-me-the-reverse-psychology-of-likeability/?sh=c1d4bb674a57

[10] Franklin B., *The Autobiography of Benjamin Franklin*, Classic Books

[11] Carnegie D., *How to Win Friends and Influence People*, Simon & Schuster

[12] Gottesfeld A., "Fail Better," *Princeton Alumni Weekly*, https://www.princeton.edu/~paw/columns/on_the_campus/on_the_campus_060607.html

[13] Komisar R., "Goodbye Career, Hello Success," *Harvard Business*

Review, https://hbr.org/2000/03/goodbye-career-hello-success

[14] "E. St. Elmo Lewis," *Wikipedia*, https://en.wikipedia.org/wiki/E._St._Elmo_Lewis

[15] "Shawshank Redemption, 'Do you trust your wife?'," *YouTube*, https://youtu.be/IZp2Ovy5pwQ?si=cT6ohXXZOI_BGXXc

[16] Halbert G., *The Boron Letters*

[17] Pink D., *To Sell Is Human*, Riverhead Books

[18] Provost G., *100 Ways to Improve Your Writing*, Berkley

[19] "Bystander Effect," *Psychology Today*, https://www.psychologytoday.com/us/basics/bystander-effect

[20] Wright E., "Understanding Readability Scores," *Erin Wright Writing*, https://erinwrightwriting.com/understanding-readability-scores

[21] "120 Years of Literacy," *National Center for Educational Statistics*, https://nces.ed.gov/naal/lit_history.asp

[22] Zipkin N., "Looking for Inspiration? All It Takes Is 6 Words," *Entrepreneur*, https://www.entrepreneur.com/living/looking-for-inspiration-all-it-takes-is-6-words/252918

[23] Isaacson W. and Bezos J., *Invent and Wander: The Collected Writings of Jeff Bezos*, Harvard Business Review Press

[24] Palahniuk C., *Consider This: Moments in My Writing Life after Which Everything Was Different*, Grand Central Publishing

[25] Voss C., *Never Split the Difference: Negotiating If Your Life Depended On It*, Harper Business

[26] Burgis L., *Wanting: The Power of Mimetic Desire in Everyday Life*, St. Martin's Press

[27] Jorgenson E., *Almanack of Naval Ravikant: A Guide to Wealth and Happiness*, Magrathea Publishing

[28] Swanson A., "Kurt Vonnegut graphed the world's most popular stories," *Washington Post*, https://www.washingtonpost.com/news/wonk/wp/2015/02/09/kurt-vonnegut-graphed-the-worlds-most-popular-stories/

[29] Altucher J., "The Idea Matrix – What Changed Everyone's Life After 'Choose Yourself'," https://jamesaltucher.com/blog/the-idea-matrix-what-changed-everyones-life-after-choose-yourself/

[30] Leddy G., "The Power of 'Thanks'," *Harvard Gazette*, https://

news.harvard.edu/gazette/story/2013/03/the-power-of-thanks/

[31] "Alec Baldwin's 'Glengarry Glen Ross' Sales Monologue | 'Third prize is you're fired.'," *YouTube*, https://youtu.be/W4we4qGiBrg?si=N112fASXeTD6AuvY

[32] Flynn D., "the idol effect," *Win with Flynn*, https://winwithflynn.com/2023/04/03/the-idol-effect/

[33] Pressfield S., "Resistance Thrives in Darkness," *Steven Pressfield*, https://stevenpressfield.com/2023/05/resistance-thrives-in-darkness-2/

[34] Freedman J.L. and Fraser S.C., "Compliance without pressure: The foot-in-the-door technique," *APA PsycNet*, https://psycnet.apa.org/doiLanding?doi=10.1037%2Fh0023552

[35] "Carrie Underwood | 'I have the ability to cluck like a chicken,'" *YouTube*, https://youtu.be/nrwTjzK4RN4?si=oslNgODJGcVL-hzn

[36] Feldman Barrett L., "This is how your brain makes your mind," *MIT Technology Review*, https://www.technologyreview.com/2021/08/25/1031432/what-is-mind-brain-body-connection/

[37] "The Tim Ferriss Show Transcripts: Neuroscientist David Eagleman — Exploring Consciousness, Sensory Augmentation, The Lazy Susan Method of Extraordinary Productivity, Dreaming, Improving Hearing with a Wristband, Synesthesia, Stretching Time with Novelty, Lessons from Titans of Science, and Much More (#674)," *The Blog of Author Tim Ferriss*, https://tim.blog/2023/05/29/david-eagleman-transcript/

[38] Kershner K. and Henderson A., "What's the Baader-Meinhof Phenomenon," *howstuffworks*, https://science.howstuffworks.com/life/inside-the-mind/human-brain/baader-meinhof-phenomenon.htm

Made in United States
Troutdale, OR
04/01/2024

18860213R00097